THE KEYS TO THE KINGDOM

From
The GREAT BROTHERHOOD OF LIGHT

EDITH BRUCE

ISBN 0-929385-94-2

Published by
Light Technology
Publishing
P.O. Box 1526
Sedona, AZ 86339
1 (800) 450-0985

printed by
MISSION POSSIBLE
Commercial Printing
P.O. Box 1495
Sedona, AZ 86339

THE KEYS TO THE KINGDOM

from the
GREAT BROTHERHOOD OF LIGHT
EDITH BRUCE

Acknowledgments

I would like to thank Muriel and Bill Williams and Trisha Cochrane for their support in producing this book. And especially my gratitude goes out to

John McIntosh,

who gathered the material, transcribed, edited and assembled the contents of this book from the many readings given through me by the Brotherhood of Light.

Preface

This little book, spiritually rich in wisdom and timely in terms of current world changes, has been assembled from a series of channeled readings given through the Rev. Edith Bruce by The Great Brother/Sisterhood of Light as outlined in detail later. These readings were then reconstructed in such a manner as to provide continuity.

Nevertheless, each chapter and each subsection within each chapter stands on its own merit and can be read and studied by itself for whatever benefit it may provide the reader.

Therefore it is suggested when reading this book, in order to gain maximum personal advantage, small portions be studied and digested before proceeding to the next. This is of particular importance for those who are new to this area of philosophy.

Additionally, an intuitive method of reading tiny sections at a time can have almost miraculous results. This is a simple procedure that works as follows; think of a question or concern you may have and then ask your higher self to provide you with the answer. Then with your eyes closed flip through the pages of the book at random, stopping when you feel influenced to do so, and read whatever portion provides the reply you require. Try this little intuitive method of reading as often as you like and judge the results for yourself.

Contents

Foreword

The truth of a life well lived is simple; it always has been. Throughout mankind's history, the Father/Mother God's guiding light has shone through a band of humble yet powerful brothers and sisters, masters all. The Great Brother/Sisterhood of Light has shone the light of its love throughout the world during all of its evolution. Most of its loving membership has remained beyond the shadowy veil of mankind's consciousness, but here and there its presence has been felt directly on the Earth plane.

Usually hidden away from the chaos and darkness of the world's busy highways and byways, the masters have remained anonymous to all but a few worthy souls who have dedicated themselves selflessly to the laws of love and truth, and have served humanity humbly in a thousand different ways throughout history. These are the disciples of the masters, souls who act as instruments stepping down the powerful frequencies of pure love into digestible portions that mankind can use to brighten its way along the journey home to the Christ consciousness. One such soul is Edith Bruce, who has worked tirelessly and humbly in the Father's service since her late teens and continues now into her eighties.

The humble teachings offered in this revealing little book represent the simple but powerful guidance given by the Brotherhood of Light through Edith Bruce for over sixty years. Her life has been a shining model of the life exemplified by the Master Jesus the Christ. Thousands have been touched by her simple yet powerful manner, and they are always struck by the deep humility with which she performs her daily service. If ever a soul represented a pure life devoid of selfish ego, it is the life of Edith Bruce.

Edith works as a trance medium, allowing high spiritual masters to flow through her and perform the Father's work. Today this method of spiritual work is referred to as *spiritual channeling*. This alludes to an individual who is sensitive and receptive to spiritual inspirations and acts as a channel for that inspiration to be expressed in the physical world. This process is usually verbal, but can extend into other creative expressions, particularly in a variety of artistic endeavors. Edith, however, is not conscious of the communication as are most channelers are today. Edith's consciousness leaves her body when she goes into a trance state and one or more of the masters communicates through her.

To the uninitiated this conjures up dark rooms, moaning sounds in the distance, shadowy figures and mumbo-jumbo. That might well be true of many who abuse the gullible by pretending to have access to higher spiritual guidance. Nothing could be further from the truth in the case of Edith Bruce. I have been her student and friend for over twenty years and have never witnessed anything but the most beautiful, uplifting and effective healing service from a union of wise and loving souls flowing through a humble servant to assist all who ask for help. And I have never known her to turn anyone away, often at the expense of her own rest and comfort. As she recently told me, "The need is so great today!" The service that Edith has rendered for over sixty years could be available only to a soul who has attained sufficient humility and spiritual awareness to access the invaluable assistance that is available from our elder brothers and sisters of light.

It has been my great honor and privilege to act as transcriber for my beloved teacher of over twenty years, Edith Bruce, in the compilation of these beautiful truths into this little book.

— John McIntosh, author of *The Millennium Tablets*

A Biography of Edith Bruce

Reverend Edith Bruce was born Edith Douglas on the 15th of February, 1914, in Aberdeen, Scotland. Her mother, whose family name was Innes, was the great-granddaughter of Lord Lovat, linking her to the Scottish aristocracy.

Her father died when she was barely two years of age, and a few years later her mother became ill and was unable to support or care for her six children. The family unit was split up and Edith, at the tender age of five, was sent to a foster family that owned a farm. This would be her home for the next nine years. During this period, while attending school and working on the farm, she recollects seeing faces in the sky and feeling the spirit presence of her father close by. Although she was regarded as a dreamer and little attention was paid to her "childish fantasies," the special gifts she would later share with the world were slowly emerging.

At age fifteen Edith returned to her mother's home. During this period, accompanied by her mother, she encountered her first communication with spirit at a Spiritualist meeting. Here she had a definite spirit communication with her deceased father.

Edith continued to develop her psychic gift, and it was not long before her marvelous psychic ability was recognized. By the time she was eighteen she was devoting all of her free time voluntarily to healing those in need. During a healing session at this time she had her first experience of trance mediumship when she was suddenly taken over by her spirit guide, Abdul (known as Nadai), who has been her constant administrator throughout her lifetime. He was later joined by another spirit known as Sebu, a spirit healer for bones and body alignment.

In 1935, Edith, now twenty-one, married George Bruce, a registered nurse. Two years later their daughter May was born. Edith continued her spiritual healing, establishing her own ministry and church in 1945, which was known as the Temple of Light. Here she was able to communicate spirit philosophies and messages from spirit to a much larger congregation. By now her lifelong association with a master spirit guide was firmly established — Han Wan by name, a philosopher of the highest order and teacher of wisdom.

A new horizon opened up for Edith when May, now married, settled in Toronto, Canada, with her husband. Before long Edith was a seasoned transatlantic traveler. Eager to fulfill the need for her special gifts, she accepted invitations to administer at different churches that upheld the practice of spiritual healing and spiritual philosophies. In honor of her dedication and service to the community she was in due course ordained as a reverend by the Britton Memorial Church.

In 1978 the Rev. Edith Bruce, with husband George by her side, gave up her church in Aberdeen and started a new chapter in her life in Toronto at the age of sixty-four.

Reverend Edith is now eighty-two years of age. Her healing ministry has taken her the length and breadth of Canada and the United States. Through her spiritual work she has bonded friendships far and wide. Thousands have benefited from her loving kindness and her healing touch. She spends each day ministering to all who need her help, and they are many. She is the living inspirational proof of all that she teaches.

In 1954 the master Abdul Nadai materialized before Edith and gave her the blueprint of the life she had come to live, saying, *"I have come a long way to get here and much I have lost on the way. My name is Abdul, but I will always be Nadai to you as a nom de plume. I have watched over you from your tenderest of years until you reached the age to be used by spirit. You did not come with worldly wisdom in this lifetime; you came as an empty vehicle to be used by spirit. We do not allow you to read books of man's ideas; only that which is authentic will you give. Your work in this lifetime is to give philosophy, healing and spiritual upliftment. You will touch not hundreds, but thousands — but you will never know what you do. You will always hold the humility, but when you return to spirit you will see what you have accomplished. I will come again."* Edith's face lights up with a smile as she says, referring to this last statement, "So . . . I'm still waiting." Those who have been privileged to know her have been truly blessed.

A Brief Biography of Han Won

Han Won lived in China about 200 years before the birth of Christ. He was a master of the ancient wisdom and, as he has told me (John McIntosh), held the keys to all wisdom, power and love. At that time Edith, through whom he has channeled philosophy for over 50 years, was his niece and student. He left the earth for the last time in that incarnation through assassination. He foretold his death at the hands of those in power, who wanted the keys he possessed. Because he would not give them up, he was stabbed in the back. That was his transition.

Although Han Won lived about the time of the Buddha and embraces all great spiritual philosophies through the thread that links them, his talks lean heavily toward the Christ teachings. However, he acknowledges a hierarchy of masters who have taught in every great school throughout mankind's history and who form what is referred to as the Great Brother/Sisterhood of Light.

Opening Prayer

Beloved Heavenly Father, as we knock on the higher door I humbly ask that we be sweetly overshadowed by the powers that be, and that the energies flow all around us from the master healers that be and those of the wisdom. May their power be energized to the needs of my brothers and sisters who will read these words.

May the Master's influence also be with us so that we might be given the inspiration and the aspiration in the work that lies before us for the New Age. May the new Aquarian Age be brought in with a greater love and humanitarian power.

I now ask to be that humble servant that might be used by those higher masters. May all that is given now, Father, be pleasing unto thee, and may the Master lead us and inspire those who are important to the future needs of the world. I ask it in thy holy name and give unto thee the full praise, the honor and glory for all that is given through love. Amen.

Edith Bruce

The Great Brotherhood of Light

Greeting from the Master Han Wan

Greetings unto you. As I come down the great stairway I cloak you in all energy and power. I am that humble master drawn in to unveil and unravel the wisdom we wish to be imparted in this book for the good of mankind and the future.

In your world today there is darkness; therefore may the rays of the spiritual sun penetrate the clouds to give refreshment to all who are seeking, all who are heavy laden and all who have heavy hearts. May God lift their souls to light and harmony that they may understand and try to unravel the confusion in their lives and gather God's wisdom that is there for all who seek, if only humanity will open to its higher self through the portals of higher wisdom.

There are many portals, soul centers within each of

us. I ask that the Master's blessings be transmitted to this book, and may all that is given bring knowledge and understanding to every soul who reads it. May it be illumined in light, and may power, wisdom, healing, peace and happiness be given unto every mind and soul. May His peace generate and vibrate out to help all those who are trying to help themselves. And may His peace be upon you and yours.

I ask now, Father, to be a humble servant used by your higher masters, the ambassadors of wisdom, and may all that is given out be pleasing in thy holy sight. I ask it in Jesus' name as I give unto the Father the full praise, the honor and the glory for all things given through love. Amen.

❖

What Is
the Great Brotherhood of Light?

The Great Brotherhood of Light consists of the high masters who vibrate into the world. They are part of God's angelic force. They represent great power and respond to certain needs of the world. Where there are great needs they gather together on the higher planes of spirit, where they meet with other spirit forces who have the ability to leave their physical bodies.

For example, in certain countries in the Far East people are very close to spirit. There are certain lamas and East Indians who can leave their bodies when it is required. They are taught from their childhood and are taken by masters who teach them how to pray and release the mind of materialism. Eventually those souls become masters themselves who lead their people. They are sometimes referred to as the Masters of the Far East.

They are kept apart from all the disturbances of the material world to develop and hold within themselves the great love and light of the Father/God. And with their mastery of the material world they can leave their physical body for a time and move their spirit so that it ascends into a different vibration that is able to communicate on a higher level of life. They acquire their wisdom from masters on the spirit planes who impress their subconscious minds and thereby pass on this wisdom to people of the physical world in service.

Throughout the ages the Brotherhood of Light has been part of God's angelic force that overshadows the Earth and helps many souls cloaked in the material body who have come at this time into the physical world to help show mankind life the way it should be lived, how to live in light and how to obey God's laws.

These beings are shown how to stretch forth their hands further into the healing energies of the spiritual, mental and physical vibrations so that there is an opening from the portals of spirituality to the material mind of humanity. In this way new life and waves of cosmic energies are imparted to mankind. These souls learn not to abuse God's laws but to use those laws with wisdom and humility. They become gentle souls inspired to impart light and understanding to all who are brought into their vibrations.

The Brotherhood of Light is comprised of the masters who have the higher spiritual energies. They radiate divine, spiritual love and new life, and they have the power to ignite a spark within those who search for the light. Those ones shall not be left wanting. They will drink from the cosmic stream of life and be filled, to go on their way rejoicing, knowing beyond a doubt that God is good and is a refuge and a strength.

He will give unto all according to their different needs. As they ask, so shall they receive. The Master, too, can come in many disguises wearing many different cloaks to fit the purpose of his mission. And when He comes He gives an energy that will feed a soul and help to that soul's mental attitude and construct a life that leads to a greater spiritual accomplishment.

These higher beings work in the spirit, but are in the physical when they are needed. They work in various fields of service. I am now speaking of my brothers here with me now — Abdul Nadai and Sebu, together with all the band of healers and helpers who have the power to assist. They are with the Master, helping in places where people are being brutally attacked and have nothing to defend themselves with. They are working in places where people have been murdered, taking these souls to the other side and making bridges of light to help them get home.

In some cases when it is not a soul's time of transition, a master might step in and give assistance. The soul might have greater things still to do, and might have experienced the traumatic event to assist their future work.

Mother Mary is also very active throughout the world today. She is doing the work she knows. Because of the great travail she endured when her son was crucified on the cross, she has great compassion for the souls who suffer sadistic torture. She knows their suffering and comes here and there to spread comfort. It is no fantasy that she is seen in many places upon the Earth, bringing healing and blessing to all wherever she goes. She is also trying to show that there is a link between the spirit and the material world that is real.

This is one of the ways that spirit is using now to generate a wake-up call to reality before it is too late. There is no use crying out after all control has been taken out of mankind's hands. It is in the now when you can make or mar life. You can put your minds together with spiritual light and love and pray for peace on Earth and goodwill to all mankind so that the world can be saved from much of the destruction that is coming.

❖

The Master Han Wan

"I was in your world, too. I was a master in that time and held the ancient scrolls of wisdom and power. In another sector of my country there were those who would have abused the power of the scrolls and destroyed my people. Because I would not disclose their secrets, I was assassinated; they stabbed me from behind.

"It was not my life, but the scrolls that were important. I knew the thoughts of those who would have abused the secrets of the scrolls and prepared my successor to take my place as leader of my temple near the Great Wall of China if I did not return. That was well over two thousand years ago, before the Buddha.

"I represented the yellow rose of China, the heart lotus. The scrolls are the spiritual secrets, which are part physical and part spiritual. I was a teacher of philosophy and taught the evolvement of the soul through reincarnation into the Earth school. That was my last incarnation. It was my mission to come as a teacher. My life was not important, as I say, but the scrolls were."

The Master Nadai

My people call him Nadai, but his real name is Abdul. He also goes back over two thousand years. He was a leader of his people in Egypt, where he helped many people and possessed the inner knowledge and wisdom. He wore the star jewel on his forehead and the sacred ankh around his neck. He was a leader devoted to his religion and lived before the

Master's time.

His service extended into the worlds of the opened third eye: "If your eye be single, your whole body will be full of light" — the inward sight that few possessed in his time. His understanding of reincarnation, spiritual unity and healing were shared with his people and helped them a great deal. At that time he rode a beautiful white stallion, which he still has in the planes of spirit.

Abdul, referring to his last incarnation, says, "In our temples we had music and used certain notes or tones that would respond to the needs of the body and the mind. In those times man was nearer to God, respected the laws of love and looked to the heavens for guidance and help. So the people used certain sound vibrations that helped heal. They had their times for prayer, and no matter what their work was, they would not miss that time. They knelt in the fields to pray at those hours.

"All of that has been lost and forgotten, yet it will come back in your time when the Word will be transformed and brought back into the light, love and humanitarian ways of humility, with the grace of God imprinted in mankind's forehead where the mind is, and the third eye will receive the divinity of God and Christ.

"In my early years on the Earth plane music was widely used for healing. I was a healer and leader of my people, having learned all spiritual things. I respected all my people and taught them all I knew. I spent much time in the temples to ensure that everything that was recorded was the way I had been shown, as I possessed true spirituality.

"In the mystery schools of Egypt, God gave me the spiritual initiation that at that time was given to very few. I had to go into the bowels of the Earth with only a few sips of water to last many days. Through the many tests of endurance I became a master of the divinity of God's power and was given a certain identity, which is the star on my forehead.

"So I took my decrees, never abusing the powers given to me that allowed me to heal and pass on the teachings of the soul. I am close to the Master in many, many ways. The work I do now emanates from the purity, the spiritual and divine love for mankind. It involves healing the sick, uplifting the depressed and those who are weak of flesh.

"We masters try to convert them into the fold like the stray lambs from the flock. That is the calling needed today to bring the lambs and the sheep together, one family under one God who is almighty, all-powerful and wonderful. We are shown His wonders so often and in so many ways, if only mankind would open its eyes to behold the light and the truth.

"We love each and every soul. And each one has the same opportunity to seek spiritual progress in the halls of learning, wisdom, music, art and medicine, which are far greater in our world than on the Earth plane.

Even the masters who help those in the Earth school are being helped by still higher masters and continue to take higher and higher spiritual initiations.

"Masters also help those on the material plane to take their initiations. These souls are inspired by masters to help give them the talent they need with the right balance in mind and sincerity of heart for what they are seeking to achieve, no matter what their path is. No one is ever alone! God then gives them the exact wisdom they require through those portals or openings in the mind that have been stimulated to accept and receive God's light. Thus they can make the correct decisions.

"There are some souls who are unaware of the source of their inspiration, yet they are doing God's work. In order for their work to be completely fulfilled and to have the inspired radiation that is the mark of an awakened spiritual person, this understanding must one day come to them.

"It is like dotting the i's, crossing the t's and adding the punctuation, to bring an inspired piece of writing to successful fruition. It is like a piece of beautiful music that lacks rhythm and is therefore not whole. Music is color and energy, and if it is it incomplete it does not possess the radiation to inspire the same results.

"I now work very much with the Master in war-torn areas of the world where I help those who are cast out of the light through traumatic circumstances and do not know where they are or where they are meant to go. I help to heal their shattered consciousness and lead them out of the material world back into the light of their true spiritual home. My instrument (Edith Bruce), my vehicle in this material world, will also return to me in my realm in time."

The Master Sebu

Sebu also goes way back and was in Africa. His people lived a very simple life in mud huts. He worked with herbs and had much power. He was a master of healing bones and helped his people by setting bones and dispensing special healing poultices and medicines as the village medicine man.

He came from a tribe of very tall people and was himself eight feet in height. That goes way back almost to the tenth century after the Master lived in the physical. At the time Sebu lived on Earth, the white man came and destroyed his people. He then willed himself back to the planes of spirit so that he could come to help the white man today from the spirit plane. He has done and is doing much good work, helping especially with difficulties of the bones.

As Sebu says, "I am happy to greet and meet with you. I wish to say that it is a long time since I have been in your school of life. I have much to do now and have great compassion for mankind. Today mankind works very hard in certain ways that abuse the body and create conditions that cause bones to become disjointed. I work with many, many souls who need adjustments, and I set bones back into their proper order. I do much in that field of service for children and for all people and all ages, bringing them relief from pain. In some cases I have been able through my treatments to help many walk again. This is what I do.

"When I was on the Earth plane I lived in Africa and looked after my people as the doctor for my village. We lived a simple life working the land, and we were vegetarians. Although I did much in that time from the planes of spirit, I am now able to serve much more in my country and throughout the world, vibrating over people.

"I have worked through the instrument I am using [Edith Bruce] since she was a young teenager. She has been a faithful servant, and we love to do God's work through her. During her service to mankind in this lifetime as a member of our group, we have been able to successfully help in the healing of many souls.

"For example, there was a young girl of six with polio who was paralyzed from the neck down and was not expected to walk again. With God's grace and love, through my instrument I was given the power to work on her body. She went to the hospital for two years, was put into a plaster cast and a harness, which I did not like. She had iron braces down her spine, straps around the body and steel down the sides of her legs. The physician said she would never walk again but only stand with the help of the braces.

"I said that through spirit I would bring back every nerve cell to her body and she would walk again. When she was twelve years of age she was able to walk with the steel braces, which gave her balance. Then I broke the harnesses; no one could understand how the steel could break. It was the spirit within that broke it. Without the harnesses she could stand well and strong, and all the nerves in her body did indeed renew themselves as I told her parents they would. This was a number of years ago. She is now very happily married with a daughter, and is able to walk aided only by a walking stick. She attended university and is now a university professor.

"We were also able to help another young fourteen-year-old girl who had been deserted in the hospital by her parents as a baby because she could not walk. We were able to help her become whole with God's help. She also gained the ability to walk, and eventually married a professional man and had a family of three children. Through God all things are possible.

"Although we work through our sister as our instrument on the Earth plane, she does not know what she does, because God does not wish her to know at this time. She has humility, which means there is no ego in the way of the work. She must be humble of spirit, having love and compassion.

"We do what we can for everyone. But now it is not necessary for me to come so often because our instrument now works on a higher level. This means that she has reached a level of spiritual attainment where she can take a higher vibrational frequency or energy that enables her to work at an elevated level of healing. She has earned this power. We can work with much more power this way and have better results.

"God sends the people to her who need her help. They are given assistance through the balance she provides. We do not look for praise; we just send love and light and are happy to greet and meet people in the way we do. But in your sleep state we can have fun and are very happy together, helping you plan how you will proceed with your daily efforts."

❖

Sister Ann

Sister Ann also works in our group; she is from the twelfth century. She comes with greetings and says she used to give all the clairvoyance messages through our instrument [Edith Bruce] in her church when she was a young woman. Then she had to leave, since our instrument was depending on her too much.

Sister Ann says, "God bless you all." She loves all people and has understanding and compassion for the needs of the world today because she too sees how man has fallen by the wayside. She prays for humanity's survival during the changes to come, and that all will be enriched and brought back to God's way. God bless you.

❖

Edith Bruce

My instrument here comes home to spirit each night and has schools to go to that she teaches in and also has other work to do. But when she returns to the Earth plane her mind is blocked so that she does not know what she has done. In this way she is shielded because we want her to keep the love and humility she has. That is the way the Master wishes her to be. It would not be good for her to know, because she would not want to return to the Earth plane but would want to come home. We cannot take her yet because there are far too many who need her on the Earth plane. She came into this lifetime to do what she does, and when she was born she had a difficult life.

She has seen the Master, who comes and goes and watches her because He knows how she has done His will, and this is something that keeps her mind aligned with the glow of light.

The Master's Presence

The Master too helps people on the physical plane, some more closely than others, you understand, depending on their level of understanding and attainment. When you get up into high levels, you need that extra boost. He gives them the extra boost because He knows they can do what He wants them to do if He gives them the additional energy that will push them over the top of their task.

The Master and we can give this help when it is needed, but you will not know that we do this, as it might affect your humility and motivate an egotistical attitude. The humbler you are, the greater the gift of help from above, because spirit knows you will not abuse it. The energy flows because you are not holding it back or destroying it through selfishness. You become a channel and the power flows through you automatically.

The idea is to purify that channel so that the light flows through perfectly. To help you with this you say, "Father, thy will be done, and may I be the instrument to let your will flow wherever thy willest it to be, and forever may it grow. May the Master lead me further into His vibrations upward and onward so that I might become a soldier of light and love, not fighting with swords but fighting battles for love, kindness, godliness and mercy to all mankind."

That's how you do it. Onward Christian soldiers, and may God bless you all and keep you in his light, wisdom and the peace which passeth all understanding. Then you will know the secrets of the sacred scrolls.

❖

Co-workers with the Masters

In your world today there are highly elevated souls who are working with the Great Brotherhood of Light. They are special but they are hidden. You get one here and there, but you do not recognize them and they do not consciously know who they are at this point. They have parts to play and they are doing their work under the supervision of a higher master who leads them.

They are taught in their sleep state and go to the halls of wisdom in the higher planes. They are recharged and have a peace that doesn't think about what is going to happen ahead. They live only one day at a time; therefore they live in the now. These souls are just like everyone else, but they have the spiritual power for which they have paid the price. They have come into the world and have chosen the same way as your own. They are living their lives; that is the part they have chosen to play for the New Age.

❖

Earth Spirits

There are spirits of the Earth that work and look after the life force of the flowers. They have angel rings in the fields of plant life. They reenergize and help all the animals, birds and wildlife, besides having a life of their own. Some souls see these spirit helpers in childhood, but as they grow they usually lose this ability because they need to live in the outside world. It is all right while they are young, but not as they grow. As the Master says, "When you grow to be a man you put away childish things." As you reach the streams you build bridges. In every walk of life there is a maturing of the mind.

❖

Help Is Always Available

Your world and your bodies are surrounded in a thick cloud of contamination both on the physical plane and above. Those who are not aware of the help always available from inner planes of spirit are vulnerable to sickness and disease when they allow these lower vibrations into their body, mind and spirit. Therefore, humankind must reach up and tune in to the higher wavelengths for protection — to rise out of these contaminations.

Everyone is vulnerable to these vibrations unless they lift their thoughts and come into God's way, into the light, for light is might. Therefore, each day cloak yourself in light and pray for that light. This will get you tuned in to your higher self, the higher powers and to the Master, who is so much in the vibrations of your world. He comes and He goes and He sees exactly what the state of the world is now.

Mother Mary, God bless her, also vibrates in your world now and is trying to help children and women who are pressured and downcast. She is comforting, supporting and guiding many. Like her son, she comes and goes throughout the world.

The Master wears many cloaks and no one knows Him. He can intermingle anywhere and observe human beings. For example, He can touch those people in need and lead them to places of rest or food or clothing and such. Those of us in the Brother/Sisterhood of Light also radiate and register our influence all over the Earth.

We too are God's sons and daughters and obey His word. He always goes with us on our missions. We can be like a cloud in the atmosphere registering our spiritual influence down to areas in need, stimulating the light and protecting those who are abused. However, if it is God's will that a conflict such as a war is to be left for humans to fight out between each other, then we must stand back. In that case we would help the wounded and those who are in danger as well as those who have been cast out of the light.

They are taken over to the spirit world because they don't know where they are. This happens when they leave the Earth plane by way of an explosion, for instance. We make bridges of light that attract them. Then they can go up and over into the planes of spirit where they are received by many servants who are dedicated to their work of service to God.

God created this world for mankind's evolvement and so that he would learn to grow, to create, to love and to share, but mankind was overpowered by materialism and lost the spiritual. But the Master said, "I will come again in a few thousand years and mankind will then bow his head to God and understand that where there is a will, there is a way, and it has to be a spiritual way.

"The spiritual way will open a gateway and then heaven will manifest the light to the world so mankind will look up to the light. Then the Father will send an influencing wave of love that will touch the souls of mankind, restoring and replenishing its spiritual identity that is cleansed of all the weaknesses of the lower self. And mankind will reach up to the higher self, loving God and loving his neighbor as himself. All shall give and take and compromise so that prosperity will spread over the entire world, not just in portions here and there. And that is how it will be."

Higher Guidance

Each soul has a guardian angel who is dedicated to you from before you touch the Earth plane. That soul is with you from the beginning of life. It takes you to the spirit plane each night and brings you back into your body after your sleep state is completed.

Sometimes they have to push you in because you wish to stay on the spirit plane. You might say, "Why should I go back to the Earth plane when I am so happy here?" But you have missions to perform and a blueprint to complete, so the guardian angel has to be strong and bring you back, sometimes with a sudden jerk. You wonder, "Where have I been, what has happened?" That is because you had to be forcefully put back into your physical body.

Understand that no damage is done to the soul; the door had to be opened and they had to push you back. That is one of their duties. Then they cloak you in energy and bless you. You might feel frustrated when you get up in the morning and find yourself a little off-balance, perhaps not in the best of temper. This is because you did not wish to come back into your physical shell and are reacting to being taken from the joy, happiness and experience of being with loved ones.

Once you are back in your body you are fine, but the guardian angel sometimes must be strong to put you there. I know that many have had that experience. I feel that it is important just to know that your guardian angel does have a very important part to play in your life and that he watches over you. But he has nothing to do with your Earth life pattern because that guidance comes from a higher master from another energy plane.

You can accept or disregard the guidance of your higher master, who helps you with your life pattern, but if you refuse to do what the master wishes, he has to stand back and allow you free will and let you continue what you are doing. Free will must be given, and afterward you have your regrets and your repentance. Then he helps you when you cry out for help and guidance — but you have learned something.

He will help you in any way he can to put things in order. As you progress and prosper with more knowledge, you draw other higher masters to help guide your evolvement, but the higher master who was originally with you still remains by your side.

The lower impulses are not spiritual; they exhibit

anger, resentment and confusion, a desire to show what they will do and how they can do it so that others will notice them. This is not using the higher self, which feeds the outer mind — and that's what brings confusion. The lower self is impulsive, and often when people have listened to it they say, "But I thought I was doing the right thing."

When you are impulsive you might feel that's what you want to do, although it is not the right thing to do. When you listen to the lower impulses, there is greed and ego involved. You attract forces of the lower planes on this physical world and the spiritual world, which make the results worse. This draws the lower entities who would use you; then they leave you to take responsibility for what has occurred. The soul becomes obsessed when it opens the door to lower forces.

At this time your world is so black and heavy with the clouds of negativity that there is no spirituality. Mankind does not wear a cloak of light and ask for God's protection; it feels it knows it all and therefore uses the ego. As a result there are many catastrophes happening in your world today and they will continue to happen until conditions bring mankind to its knees one way or the other.

You need to cloak your homes in light. God is your refuge as He is your strength, and the Master is also registering His power and His light in the atmosphere. The cosmic energy is a God-power full of everything that is wonderful and good, if you will only reach up and absorb it in union with God, His spirit forces and with the Master who is so much in your world at this time, helping to lift so many souls who have been abused and restoring light to their lives so that they will also be servants of the light.

It is through God's laws, not man's, that people see the light and feel comfort, which renews their faith, hope, courage and sense of humility. In this way they will be restored and strengthened by what they have endured. Mankind has a great deal to learn and much to give back in return for what it has taken for granted. The stresses and pressures of your world are far greater than they have ever been and mankind is more vulnerable than ever before.

You must keep in constant contact with spirit and protect yourselves and others, as God is your refuge and your strength. Knock on the door with humility and it will open.

❖

2

Earth Changes

The World Is Now Reaping What It Has Sown

Humanity must now open its eyes, behold the circumstances that surround it and begin to realize that great changes are ahead. The world is going through much travail, and every country of the world will have its problems and upheavals, some more than others.

Humans have to become aware of their own soul and of their true being — that they are spirit incarnate. They need to learn to open their inner portals and see the world in its current state of rupture. They need to know also that this condition is not God's way. Humans have created this situation through their own choices, because they have not shown respect for the planet for a very long time.

Mankind has been given too much, yet demands more. Some are respectful, but many wish to gather the harvest before it is ripe. This is where the world is out of alignment.

As it is written in your holy book, Revelations, God would smite the Earth and would shake its foundations if humanity does not stop and see the catastrophe it is causing the Earth. It has polluted the Earth through toxic materials put on the soil to increase the speed and yield of crops, but the seeds are contaminated through the use of these poisons. This practice has contaminated the entire Earth.

Over the years these toxic materials have been cycled and recycled until the value of the soil has been greatly reduced. In addition, the atmosphere is polluted through a multitude of contaminating gases. The evil of greed has sought materialism only and not respected the spiritual aspect of the Earth.

Mankind can see that the trees are not as fruitful and the fields are not producing the same foods they used to. Nor is the food as nutritious, because your soil is contaminated. You no longer have luscious fruits or vegetables as before. This is mankind's doing and will remain as it is until that time when the Lord will cleanse the world and restore the Earth to virgin soil in much the same way that you would cleanse your body.

God sees the evil of humanity's greed and the brutalities it inflicts on animals, for they too have endured great suffering at man's hand. As a consequence the world is out of balance.

Mankind has no respect for God's creations, with

the result that it has caused untold suffering and generated much fear, which is now reflecting back on mankind.

Now God is gradually taking the reins of power out of humanity's hands to observe whether it will see the light and wake up to the reality of what it is doing. As He said, "I will shake the very foundation of the world, the Earth, and blood will flow like a river" — which He has and is still doing. But afterward He will make a new Earth.

From this time on, it is *now* that you are into the great travails. But after the times of trouble you will see the return of the Master.

Where to Expect Some Changes

Observe how much different the human body is than it ever was before. A great many of the changes are of mankind's own creation through its way of life and consumption of contaminated food. There is no energy in it, for it has been contaminated through the chemicals mankind has put into the soil. It is bad for the body and bad for the blood.

There is something to be said for fertilizing the ground naturally with manure; that is the right way. Contamination does not always show up right away, perhaps not for a year, two years or even a number of years, but once it overwhelms the soil, it goes fast. That is why there is so much contamination now.

Your bread is contaminated because the wheat has been grown with so many chemicals due to the desire for a big harvest and a larger monetary return, rather than for the good of the body.

The acquisition of material things has become an obsession and has destroyed God's world. God has allowed it to go its full limit, but soon He will have to take back the controls. As a result, soon you will see natural catastrophes in many parts of the world.

In Vancouver, Canada, there will be turbulence and big volcanic eruptions. In Toronto you will have floods and quakes in the lakes, flooding well into the middle of the city. There will also be other problems: terrific winds will cause a lot of damage.

Other areas that will experience flooding and quakes are Orlando, Florida, and in and around the lake areas in that state. Also, New York will have floods and quakes. San Francisco too will have quakes, and that city will disappear as will other parts of California.

Some parts of the world that have once been lost beneath the waters will rise, and the face of the world will be changed — a new Earth for the new world.

Japan will also have big quakes. They have had some already, but there are more to come. China, too, will have its problems, along with Mexico, Africa and India — all are in for large quakes. London will also get quakes, with much flooding and water damage. The Thames will overflow its banks, causing floods near the Parliament buildings. Scotland will have similar problems. Other parts of the world will have disease, floods and earthquakes. Many places where land meets the water will have high winds and upheavals. That is how I see it.

Prepare Now

As this happens there will be a big ball of light that will go through the atmosphere. It will cleanse the Earth after all your upheavals are finished. You will have floods, earthquakes and typhoon winds; all these will come, but not all at once. The world will change, your atmosphere will change, your seasons will not be as they were in the past. You will get a varied mix. These will affect the crops and the land, and there will not be the same food.

So people must prepare with dried foods to take them through a period that could last perhaps a year, perhaps longer. Dried foods will keep; that is why it is being given to those who will be left, so they will have their needs met when food is not so easily attainable. This is important now. You also need dried milk and salt, dried chicken, fish and potatoes. In places they are plentiful. Many people are preparing themselves now so that they will not be wanting.

You must also put your homes in good condition so that you have heat, because you will not always have the light you have now. Your energy will change when you have storms, so you will need to have supplies to make fires and light: wood, oil or kerosene or candles. You will need three sets of woolen clothes for changes, which is very important, as well as quilted sleeping bags for when there is no heat, and also rubber boots. It's not how you look, but how warm you are that counts.

These are the things that are important for survival. You could have one-piece outfits to keep warm, especially for those who must go out in the cold frequently. You will also need medications — for example, oils for use on dry skin, like castor oil or olive oil. If you do those things God will look after you, and you can help one another.

But do not let your right hand know what your left hand has and vice versa, meaning do not tell people what you have because certain people would steal from you. These are the simple things you have to be aware of to secure your homes and your lives. Then God will look after you and yours.

Protecting You and Yours

When Earth changes come, some people might become desperate to survive at any cost. Naturally you have to defend yourself, but hold your faith strong and pray and say, "Father, may Thy will be upon my will and may I and my loved ones be protected. May my home be protected; may no entity be allowed to come into my home to abuse or misuse it, and may my family be held in safekeeping." That is how you protect yourself and your loved ones.

If you have weapons and someone were to invade your privacy, they might get the weapon and use it on you. Then what would you do? If you live by the sword, you will die by the sword. God is your refuge and your strength. The Master knows His own and will guide and protect them.

The Influence of Fear

As the Earth changes increase and become more difficult to deny, there will be many who do not understand and will become greatly agitated. There will be some who will wish to end the fear through the taking of their own lives. But what is to be will be. God knows all. If it is their time to go, you can do nothing to stop that; you can only do what you know how to. That is how it is.

God is their strength and their refuge. Each soul has a blueprint or life pattern, and each has a time of transition.

The Forerunners

Those who are prepared, who know what is coming and have certain knowledge, will be the forerunners. They will be in the forefront and will calm the minds of those who are in a state of panic. They will encourage and inspire these disturbed souls to have faith and know that help is available. They will be shown also that all must be disciplined, not pushing and shoving, so that all can be given their portions under the circumstances of the times until things are brought into order.

The angels will overshadow each and every soul and will put their powers over the minds of all. There will be peace and trust and faith and courage through the turbulent times, and each will help the other so that no one will be alone.

Each soul must learn to obey God's laws because they have abused them for so long. The Lord has been patient, very patient. It is running very close to the time when the disasters will lead to peace, and then you will see God's way.

Wake Up and See the Signs

This is a time when a lot of people are sitting on the fence. They do not deny that changes are happening, but they do not accept them because they don't understand and are bewildered and afraid. They don't want to accept that such things can happen. Why would God do this? they ask themselves. Why would He not stop the world from heading into greater catastrophes?

Usually these souls need both a little push and a little pull. It's just like medicine: Sometimes you have to take a medication to correct a condition of stagnation and activate the system. The mind has to be taken out of its stalemate and shown the ruptures, discord and disasters occurring all over the world so that it can comprehend the great suffering the Earth is currently experiencing.

Often, however, mankind sees all the brutalities and degradation going on in the world, but doesn't want to get involved. It's as if it is saying, "As long as I'm all right, why should I get entangled?" But that is not the way to look at it.

Spirit is trying to reach mankind with messages from many sources, from appearances in many places of high masters such as Mother Mary, through many different methods such as books like this, to thousands of near-death experiences all over the world, to a multitude of reported miracles (such as a child surviving after days buried under a bombed-out building). This is spirit giving mankind light, showing it through various situations that there is a greater power beyond, and that this power is the God power. God has His ambassadors and soldiers of light; they are the ones doing the good deeds and will continue to do so, but mankind has to wake up to the fact that if it is sitting on the fence when the floods of change come, it will have to move or be swept away.

Mankind has to wake up now to the value that lies within and ask, "What am I here for?" and not stand on a fence doing nothing when others are trying to do their best. People must say instead, "I must join in the band and pursue my higher potential, igniting the energy of light and wisdom within myself," then with a clear and joyful voice proclaim that new awareness from the highest rooftop.

Then God will say, "At last I have awakened my children of the Earth to a greater identity of life where love now can be used and not abused, where through the igniting of that pure love they will be bonded together. And through caring, sharing and protecting the light of truth, the world will be put back into its network of peace and harmony and good will and health to all mankind will be restored."

And in that time every country will be bonded in that love, in tune with God's power. When humanity knocks on the Father's door, He will hear and they will receive things that are good for their souls' advancement.

At that time the Master, the Christ, will shepherd the people and help them to find their balance, their needs of life, thus help bring them into a state of wholeness. Once the Earth is put onto a smooth foundation with peace and goodwill to all mankind, all shall have happy thoughts and happy days, and they will have learned to walk the pathways of respect for one another. They will gather knowledge and understanding, learning never to abuse or misuse anyone. They will have a sense of peace such that when they lay their head down at night they know there is nothing to fear and that there is serenity in the world and a supreme being that ignites in their soul a sense of comfort, love and peace.

They will know the reality that there is no longer any danger in the world. They will know that life is a continuity and evolves, even the animals. And that mankind evolves until it reaches God and the great spiritual grace of the Hierarchy to the source of laws where all first came from.

Look for the impulses (which are not really impulses but a voice) that tell you, "Get this, do this or go there," repeated over and over. Pay attention to them, because you are receiving that guidance or warning for a purpose, for your own benefit and security. If you don't, you are the losers because you did not listen to the guidance. You will see the signs and then you will know to prepare. It is just like seeing black clouds and knowing it's going to rain. So you prepare. It is the same with the signs that you'll see.

Don't wait until it is upon you. You have to pay attention more to things like so-called coincidences; these are forms of guidance. You must prepare yourself now for your own protection, putting your prayers out to God, asking for divine protection and guidance and always listening to the inner voice, the higher self.

Always remember the natural laws and that God is the divine Master of the world. Christ, the Master, is his counterpart, the heart of God, the love and the energies available to all who are open and receptive to His holy word. They shall be enriched in body, mind and spirit and shall not perish in the times to come. They will also know everlasting life.

Open to His presence; His energies are of faith, hope and charity, and charity will give you serenity. May God bless you and guide all His people throughout the world, through every corner of the Earth. May each and every soul be granted its portion of manna this day, and may you drink from the living well, the stream of life and cosmic love. God bless the world and hold it in His hands. God bless you.

❖

Destiny in the Balance

But now evil is very, very predominant in your world. With what we see now, anything could happen at any time; it depends on many things in the world. We cannot say such-and-such will happen on a certain day in a certain month or year, because it depends on many things in your world at this time and how the many variables unfold.

There are many evildoers who are using terrible weapons and will therefore destroy themselves, at what price we cannot say. But when God sees the world has reached the limit of evil vibrations — and that time is fast approaching — He will act, and that will be the end of it.

❖

All Things Are Not Revealed

God does not reveal all things to mankind. It would not be good for you to know everything in advance, as this would disrupt you in mind and spirit. I think it is better that you do not have the full picture in your hands because you might tamper with it by focusing on the negative things.

Things to Come

Like a Thief in the Night

There is only one God, almighty and all-powerful. Call Him what you will, there is still only one God, and when the Master returns He will once again teach this. When the world has gone through its travail and is again in a state of balance, He will come and teach the people who are even now praying for Him to return, believing He will come to lead the world back into humanitarian ways.

The Master said, "I will come again within the next two thousand years and I will come like a thief in the night. I will count my lambs and my sheep and I will go to the highways and byways and gather all who are lost. The lost sheep will be brought back into the fold. Then shall I teach them and give them the love they have been looking for. They shall drink from the living stream and be filled with joy and love and light."

He will touch the world and go where people are

waiting and praying for Him every day. He will embrace them, love them and teach the holy words of wisdom, showing them the way. Then He will go here and there all over the world teaching the philosophies of the soul and bringing back the knowledge and understanding to "love thy neighbor as thyself and to honor thy father and thy mother that thy days may be long with the land."

He will teach and give unto all new guidance and love. He is the love of God in the hearts of all mankind, and that love will be reborn in every person's heart so that there will no longer be hatred due to race, color or creed. All will be in harmony with one another, and life will be on a different level of spirituality.

And when the Master shows himself it will be to every part of every country throughout the whole world. All will be one family in the eyes of the Great Spirit. The Father/Mother/God will reveal the brotherhood of God and the brotherhood of mankind united, bounded in light and love. Mankind will know that God is light and love; the Master Christ will be the image of humanity incarnate and discarnate when they return to spirit, and much of the Christ will be in each and every one.

❖

The Ancient Scrolls

The ancient scrolls of wisdom will be revealed and will be used to put man into a state of spiritual balance through the Father/Mother/God, the creator of all life, and Jesus the Christ, the Son.

The Ten Commandments will be restored: Thou shalt not kill; six days shall you labor and do all thy work, but the seventh day is the day of the Lord and you shall hallow that day. As the six days are for work, the seventh is a day of rest for you and to all who work within your vibrations — in and around your home. Your laborers too have need of rest and prayer. Mankind will respect God's laws and bow before his God.

Then you shall find a greater peace within your souls and you will not have a thirst that you cannot satisfy. At that time you will know God's blessing, and His joy and His love will embrace you all.

A New World

Mankind will see the full extent and conclusion of the Earth eruptions and changes by the year 2000. Mankind will live in harmony, all colors and creeds. It will be a time of renewal when you will have peace on Earth, when all the prophecies of changes are fulfilled and the world will have peace for a thousand years without war.

When the ball of light goes through the atmosphere you will see a new world and a new beginning. At that time the Earth will be permeated with spirituality. Human bodies will be healed of all diseases and a new energy will be brought forth into the world that will give healthy minds and healthy bodies to all.

You will have a mind that is receptive to God's word and to the heaven world above. You will experience psychic abilities that will enable you to access the spiritual planes coming and going between the two worlds. Your consciousness will be in joy because you will have a communication with God above through the Son, who will be the mediator.

This knowledge will prove to you that you are a spiritual being incarnate in the physical world, the school of life. You will know that when you return to the spiritual world you live as a discarnate being. Your mind will be conscious of the two worlds, of the spiritual plane and of the school of life on the Earth plane, which is your base. It is the foundation you must come into periodically for your spiritual evolvement, until you reach a certain stability of spirituality which allows you to go on to higher vibrations, to dwell in the house of God and go into other realms on higher levels.

Mankind spends eons going through the cycles of life in and out of the spirit planes and the Earth-school plane to reach ascension into the planes of light through the spiritual duties of evolvement.

There will be harmony and music, exquisite sacred music that will lift your souls. People will respect one another and the Earth will return again to a state of pristine beauty. The lands will again produce abundantly, giving human minds a peace which will pass their previous understanding while enriching humans in body, mind and spirit.

You will experience a welcome relief from all stresses, pressures and discord. You will start to see and know life in a new world where there will be light, not darkness. There will be blue skies and a serenity in the atmosphere that will sparkle. The air will be heavenly with the perfumes of the ethereal essence of the flowers that will come. The trees will again flourish and cleanse the atmosphere, not as they are now, because they too are dying.

There will be no contamination, and humans as well as the animals will be healthy. You will not tear down, destroy or kill, which includes animals. You will not eat of the flesh and blood of your brother animals. The animals will have their place as well. They will have their kingdom and people will respect them. And all will be handled in humanitarian ways as it was throughout the ages. Even the birds of the air who sing their songs will be treated with respect.

You will eat of vegetables, fruits, grains and fish, such will be your diet, and thus the world will become vegetarian. And when these things are eaten they should be blessed in God's name so that they will reenergize your bodies and preserve them. The waters will be clean, clear and pure again with new forms of vegetation everywhere. These things will give you a healthy body.

To the minds that are creative, discoveries will be on a higher spiritual wave. For example, you will have vehicles that run on pure energy in harmony with all life. Water will be one of the important energies in the new Aquarian Age; this is technology you do not have at this time. However, during the rebuilding period you will return to transportation with animals.

You will live in simplicity and be loving and caring toward your fellow man. The Lord God Almighty is a God of all power, all love and all compassion, and when you walk into His arms of peace there is no pain or sorrow, but only eternal and everlasting joy and peace.

It is also very important that children too should be brought into the light of the Father/Mother God and obey their parents with love and peace. They need a pattern of direction to grow and also follow in the footsteps of the Master so that they too shall become pillars of light as they grow, respecting and obeying the laws of love. Then they will have spiritual maturity and purity within.

Their actions will speak profoundly because they will do things that are blessed from the mind and soul, feeding those who will receive the rays of God's power manifesting amongst the peoples. The children will be drawn into the ethers, the finer, higher vibrations, and there they will find peace and goodwill surrounding them. This generates a healthy mind, which then builds a healthy body.

To all the world it will be one God, almighty, all-powerful. The Father/Mother God, the giver of all good things, will overshadow His children. Then will you see humaneness for all people no matter their color or creed; it will be the brotherhood of mankind. United, all people will act together and share all that they have — yes, even a crust of bread. They will share what they have and love one another. They will use a barter system, and there will be much goodwill in the exchange of goods. No one will go without.

You will trade in peace with your fellow man when the world achieves its harmony and the Earth has been reenergized. There will be no more sickness. Your bodies will again be brought back into health, free of disease and you will experience psychic ability, which will enable you to know the two worlds.

Then as mankind unites it will give blessings to the Father, Lord God, and there will be joy and no pain or sorrow. God will move in mysterious ways amongst you and you will not fear Him but look up to Him and give praise.

In these times to come there will be those from the higher realms who will overshadow the world, manifesting and intermingling with the peoples, but they will be here today, then gone to another part tomorrow. This will continue until the world is in its perfection and all is One.

Those who are the teachers of the brotherhood of mankind are God's servants to whom he has given the

authority to administer in His name to all who will
open their eyes to behold the light and open their
hearts and soul centers, which resemble a lotus flower.
When the heart and soul are open, like the lotus they
open to receive the higher spiritual teachings.

When mankind reaches this level of spiritual recep-
tivity, the world will know the love of God in its fullest
way — almighty, all-powerful and joyful.

All religions are based on the same foundation —
love and light. Love is the path mankind must follow.
Humankind must have fellowship with its brothers, a
fellowship based on love and light, which is truth.

God is love and light, and that has to be in all individuals in every part of the world. All must embrace
each other in love and light and be at one with God. I
am not speaking of carnal love but spiritual love, a
love that is extended to all of mankind with no
thought to color or creed. It will be the beginning of
the new Aquarian Age when this concept is embedded
into the souls of mankind and there will be much love
and laughter.

The Rapture

Your world is currently going through what I call
its Gethsemane, and it will take quite a long time yet.
When it is complete, then mankind will bow before
God and say, "Enough is enough," and will seek forgiveness and remission of the suffering. Then it will

be healed and the stresses will be stopped. God will heal your distress, saying, "You will now do My will and I will make the laws." And then mankind will bow before Him and He will cleanse the atmosphere.

The mind of humanity will be healed and cleansed — this is the "rapture" you hear of in your holy book. This will give humanity joy, and all will look upon each other as brother and sister. They will praise the Lord and be enraptured by a divine love that will be instilled in their minds and soul centers.

This will activate the yellow rose of the heart, which will be expanded in purity and abound in spirituality and love for all. All will be enraptured with the atmosphere because it will be alive with spiritual purity and stir every heart and mind, correcting all minds to bring them into alignment with that spirituality. All will be enraptured in God's power and have a psychic attunement to the heart. They will have the knowledge and awareness of the spirit world and will not abuse this knowledge, but wish to do more searching within to know more. And they will be shown the way.

People will return to the land, tilling the soil, sowing seeds, and once again fruits and vegetables will grow healthy. Everyone will have all the things that are important to life. Every country, every part of the world will be of the same vibration so that they will all be stirred to serve one another. Minds will be receptive, commanding the work and focusing on living a healthy life, with each one helping the other learn the many simple ways that bring happiness.

Then you will see a wonderful world, and when people begin to show their true senses, the Master will come and teach them. He will lead them and they will have great joy. For a period of time He will take with him around the world many who will teach and bring man into at-one-ment. There will be no distinction of color or race and no discrediting of anyone. He will then visit every part of the world and bring all into a settled, happy and complete life. He will break the molds of the past ways of thinking and living.

May the Father/Mother/God bless you all and may you go forward, reaping the full harvest of what you have sown, knowing that you will have a thousand years of peace without war. Love one another as I love you now, and let no man be put out of alignment lest he lose himself. But go forward trusting and obeying the laws the Master will give to all people. By respecting these laws mankind will render service to his fellow man with joy, love and light. God is love, divine love, light, wisdom and understanding. And in that time, which will shortly be upon the world, all will have healthy minds and bodies and there will be rapturous music, happiness, peace and goodwill to all.

During these thousand years of peace without wars when brutalities have ended, mankind will have learned more and the world will be made harmonious in every way, enraptured in pure thoughts. The

Master will come and show the way; this will be your salvation.

Automatic Laws

This is the new Aquarian Age that is now just beginning, and the people who will be born into your world will be a bit different. The children coming into the world now will be of the New Age and have more spirituality. They will obey the laws that are put before them for the New Age.

The Commandments will come back, and the laws will be automatic in this way: People will know even as each is known, and nothing will be hidden. No one will be able to deceitfully say, "I didn't do this or that." They will not be allowed to look on what they did and deny it. The power will no longer be there to do that; as a result, people will obey God's laws. There are people even now who know these things.

Nadai on Health

In the area of healing there will be balance between natural medicine and conventional medicine. There have always been physicians, but today they do not always come from an attitude of humanitarianism. To be truly effective they must have compassion for suffering and take advantage of the natural healing powers of herbs, which will be widespread in the future.

In that time human bodies will be cleansed and replenished with vitality and health, and herbal treatments will be honored as an effective way to keep the body in that state of perfection. That will be the New Age. The human diet will then consist of vegetables, especially root vegetables. You will also eat and drink abundantly of fruits and fruit juices that will not be contaminated as they are today, and you will also eat fish.

Your way of life will be much more spiritual and your bodies will not be so heavy and polluted as they are today. You will have much more energy and live a life filled with peace, tranquility and divinity. There will be a sense of great happiness, and music will be one of the most important things in your life. That will be your way of life.

When a doctor works with a patient, he or she sometimes get overshadowed by a higher master or is helped from a spiritual level with the healing process. This could be a conscious request for help or could be spontaneous. It depends on the person, because each physician is quite different from others. Some are rather egotistical; then there are those who are more humble, gentle and caring. It is the latter who will draw the attention of the higher masters because the love is there. If there is no love, the assistance cannot work.

❖

Enlightenment

Life is a school of learning that leads to the evolution of the soul, and each must travel his or her path. You must drink the bitter cups, experience sacrifices and know a degree of pain and suffering. Yes, you must know heart-ache and sorrow. It is all part of the path and the journey of life.

But when you go through the river of life and finally cross it, there is the light. The illusion is behind you, and you will open to the true stream of life. When you go through that corridor there is no further desire needing to be quenched in the school of life. Thus there is no need to return because you are into a reality where you meet your loved ones and also greater minds who wish to serve you, igniting love and power in you that you too might become as they are. That is God's gift of riches to mankind's soul evolvement when it becomes anointed and open.

When your inner portals open and you become aware, you will then drink from the great stream of all energy and power and cease the creation of negative, destructive things. You will be aware that God is within your soul. You will also be conscious of the stimulation of energies needed to help you pursue a life pattern that is joyous and fruitful, allowing a much greater ease in attaining higher spiritual awakening.

❖

4

Life's Purpose

The Correct Use of Power

Everyone should pray, asking for forgiveness for all the impulses you have acted upon instead of listening to the inner voice, the higher self, through the mind, which is the motor. The mind is the controller, but many people allow the lower self, the emotions or impulses to overtake the guidance of the inner voice.

The lower self is the devil. The devil is in mankind when he allows the weaknesses of the flesh to take control. It is so simple to take the easy road, wanting everything now without working for it. Many choose to use flowery words to get what they want when they want it. Many today are like this, wearing false masks to use and abuse those they should be serving. They might sound good, but their words are just what people want to hear, hypnotizing people and taking advantage of them. Once these people get what they want, they have no more use for the faithful ones, discarding them and breaking all of their promises. The many victims of this abuse become disillusioned and feel there is no justice. They often fail to understand it is the weakness of the flesh that has been responsible for their downfall.

So I have to say, pray. Open your hearts and minds and souls and pray to the divine Father/Mother God for guidance and protection from the lower vibrations. He will lead you and send a higher master to over-shadow you and inspire and show you the way.

The Master Christ Himself can help you in this way. It is not necessary that He be beside you to do this. He can transmit waves of cosmic power to you and assist you in pursuing the right path. Working correctly through the mind instead of your impulses, you will have inspired knowledge and understanding.

Humanity must learn that the mind is the con-troller, and when you observe life unimpeded by the emotions of the lower self, you can evaluate what you are learning through the influence of the higher self. Only then can you can tap the wisdom that allows you to balance the scales of life.

In this way you climb the rungs of the ladder of spiritual evolution. From the power and strength of this level of concentration you can be more easily influenced by God, and judge what you are learning through your experiences. You begin to see the value of your life mission and appreciate what you have accomplished. This in turn strengthens your mind and your ability to create thought forms adhering to God's will. As you follow that will, you attract more light and more power of a higher nature.

Light attracts light just as dark thoughts attract dark results. When this begins to happen, a higher master is brought into your vibration to assist your development. The soul begins to gather higher knowledge, wisdom and patience with a confidence to wait and operate according to the systems that are being given through the higher self, the inner voice. As a result, you turn the wheel of growth and spiritual evolution in the correct way, not in disorder.

Soon other doors begin to open and you find that you expand and excel in the works that you are performing. You become a leader of others in your field, holding the wisdom, patience and understanding in the correct way and offering to those willing to learn. That is the process of spiritual growth.

The School of Life

One way a soul progresses is by going into the sleep state each night. The soul's master takes it to the level the person has attained spiritually. Here the master reviews the day with the soul, covering the day's tasks, what they have accomplished and the obstacles still remaining. They are shown the best ways to deal with the issues at hand and to overcome problems. This information is relayed into the subconscious mind, and in this way the soul is prepared for the next day.

This process continues each and every day so that when the soul returns to the spiritual plane each night it is reenergized and taken to a variety of places. Sometimes it will go to the halls of learning and other times to the music halls, halls of painting and art or perhaps the halls of wisdom.

The objective is that the soul will return each day with certain understanding to assist it in developing its spiritual integrity while providing for its material needs. Life is a challenge, and a soul must try to obey the laws shown to it by its master, who looks upon the soul's life pattern.

However, each soul has free will, and it may refuse to follow the guidance of its master. In these cases the master must withdraw and allow the soul to make or mar its record. If a soul makes mistakes, that is its responsibility, and this is where many fall by the way-side. This is what causes a soul to return to the Earth plane over and over again, repeating the same things until they learn and accept God's laws. Once this is accomplished and the knowledge and understanding of the laws are learned, they guard themselves with humil-ity in their daily life. This is how progress is attained.

Each of you on different levels must work out your own destiny. Whether you have a short life or a long one, you all have your own special blueprint. When your sojourn on the Earth plane is completed, you return to your true home and are shown the record of how the blueprint turned out. You cannot say you did not do this or that thing, because it is right in front of you. In this way you judge yourselves.

At this point the cry goes out where weakness and error had marred the pattern the soul had originally designed. Nothing gained on the material plane can be taken except what has been added to the soul. Into the world comes naked a soul, with only the blessing and love of God. Whatever a soul has put into its life in service to its fellow man, the sacrifices made with love and tender care is added to its spiritual bankbook; these all show you what has been built in the true home, the spiritual home. This gives true joy together with a brighter spiritual cloak of light and energy.

As the soul returns time and again, gathering more and more knowledge, understanding and wisdom, it progresses and acquires the ability to lift others who are ready to listen with interest and respect. In this way it has the opportunity to grow even faster by helping others to grow spiritually. Your world evolves in every different pattern of life through the attributes you hold, expand and extend to all countries and all peoples.

You gain understanding of different kinds by having incarnations in many different countries. Through the ups and downs of experience you gain awareness and thus greater obedience to God's direction. You become receptive to the love and care you are being given from the planes of spirit. You learn to

give and take, yet feel compassion for those less fortunate, for those who have fallen by the wayside. You
acquire compassion, lifting the less fortunate instead
of trampling the weak; you learn to offer them the
spiritual bread of life. When they thirst after righteousness you offer them the living waters of love and
compassion, for within your deepest self you realize
that you yourself once had been in their state and
would have been grateful to receive care and comfort
and a place to rest. These are the things that are amiss
today in your world.

The Result of Wasting Life's Lessons

In so many parts of the world people have become
blind to the needs of their fellow man. These
thoughtless, unkind, evil acts of brutality that are
causing untold suffering create for their perpetrators
heavy karmic debts that are imprinted on their souls
and will exact a grievous price.

Did not God create the Ten Commandments? And
what has man done with them now, broken every one?
Thou shalt not kill; honor thy father and mother that
thy days may be long upon the land with the Lord thy
God. How many respect these laws? Love thy neighbor as thyself; six days shalt thou labor and do all
thine work, except the seventh day you shall rest.

These laws are all but forgotten. All must be
washed in the blood, the life force of the Lamb, and

He will come and give you the light and the truth again. Mankind will learn the lesson of living within and respecting the laws of God; and then it will know joy and peace in life.

In your spiritual communion you go back into the planes of spirit each night with joy, embracing loved ones, not only of this life. Some go even further afield and touch great masters. They are embraced in the love and wisdom of the masters and their minds become enlightened and humbled, providing refreshment to the soul. They then go out into their Earth mission, reaching out and giving light, which attracts more light. Light attracts light and responds to love and caring through services rendered in words, in devotion and in so many different ways.

Now, this is very important to understand: You cannot know all things in one short life span. It is but a flash and then it is gone. During the Earth walk there are some who abuse those who are trying to be kind and generous. You have the false prophets who try through flowery words to misuse others, but there is no action behind their words, no root. They neither sow, spin nor grow; it is all just words and therefore they stagnate. Yet they use and abuse those who have compassion.

But when they return to the planes of spirit they find that there has been no light in their work, and they must then be placed on the spiritual plane that suits the lessons they must learn. These are the lower

astral planes where there are teachers who are protected in a cloak of light so that they cannot be
harmed in any way. These teachers bring them
through the dark and dingy vibrations clouded in
murkiness. These souls still hold their evil vibrations.

The master teachers communicate with them and
encourage them to repent their ways and come to the
light to be taught. When they do this they are brought
into the guiding light of the automatic laws, where
they are taught discipline and obedience to the laws of
light and love. In this way they slowly progress and
are then given further opportunities to enter Earth life
to continue their upward spiritual evolution.

Coming into the Earth School

There is a purpose when a child comes into the
world through one family and then is pulled away and
ends up through adoption or other means in another
family. The child has come through one door and has
to go through another for its evolvement, since there
is an affinity to its new parents.

In one way there is a sacrifice on the part of the parent who bore the child. However, the link with the
birth parent chosen by the child might be from another incarnation, and for reasons associated with the
parent's attributes the child used that parent's body or
vehicle so it could to take on some of those attributes.

In other words, there was a bond to something in

the birth parent's physical genes that was necessary for the child to use in the adopted home, and the birth parent made the sacrifice to the child on a higher level of consciousness. The deep link from the past had to be brought into the physical body of the child for reasons connected to its current spiritual growth. In this way the soul has the right body and right parents for its current journey into the school of life.

People question when life begins inside the embryo. I have to say that there is life from the moment of conception. It is in sleep state for a period of three months; nevertheless it is alive. There are cases where a soul comes into the fetus only for that experience, not intending to be born. Here you have a natural miscarriage, which is not an accident; there are no accidents.

Everything is a spiritual experience for the soul, and so it goes through the miscarriage and returns to spirit. In matters where there has been a rape or abuse that is evil, there is no harm when the fetus is aborted. You do not know what karmic condition exists, since you do not know what the soul of the mother was in a previous incarnation. Also, in cases of danger to the mother's health, abortion is acceptable.

❖

Justice: Cause and Effect

You have a time to be born and a time of transition, no matter how! That is all part of destiny. The akashic records holds all things and the angel of transition knows them. Everything has a cause and effect, and there is a purpose for all things. A soul need not wonder why it was spared and another was not in a so-called accident. In such a case it was not the soul's time to go.

Everything is just, and cause and effect touches souls through a labyrinth of possibilities. As I have said, there are no accidents and everything is in balance. You work and you live your life, but you depend on many things in your everyday living. Often you might feel, Why should this or that happen to me? What did I do to deserve this? But there is a lesson to be learned, and once it is learned it is learned forever.

With everything that comes into your life, there is an opportunity to learn a lesson to give you more knowledge and embed a deeper understanding into your life pattern.

Focused Intent

You need to think deeply about the way you grow each day, doing this one day at a time and allowing tomorrow to take care of itself. It is important to keep your focus on what you are doing until you complete your day — this day, not the next. Then you need to relax and let go and let God take over what you have put in place.

Next you prepare your body, mind and soul for

another day. When you go into your sleep state and leave your body, your guardian angel takes you to the planes of spirit where you belong. That is the level you have attained so far, and there you review your day's activities and challenges. The master who presides over you helps you unravel all your problems and puts them into perspective in your subconsciousness mind. This is where you receive inspirations during the next day as flashbacks of what you covered the night before.

You might have thought of these flashes as a sort of déjà vu. But as you come into closer and closer contact with your higher self, this work done on the inner planes will become clearer and more accessible; as you ask it will be given unto you. You will find that the power being given will register in your mind and help you to keep your balance, eliminating feelings of confusion and insecurity.

The faith and trust you have in the higher spiritual powers keeps you secure and gives you protection. It keeps you from dropping into low energies, which means you don't allow your emotions (that is, the lower self) to control you. The mind remains the controller. Your higher self feeds the mind with wisdom to give you valid understandings, not the fantasies of the lower self. Faith removes the mountain. Trust and obey, for God's way is the best way. If you do that, if you trust in the higher powers, you will not be troubled or afraid.

God never fails mankind, but mankind fails itself. God looks after His children; even to those who have gone astray will He give His love and compassion, forgiving seventy times seven, meaning that He turns the other cheek ad infinitum. May His blessings now be upon you and yours and lead you to where you will surrender to the peace and joy from the truth found in Him. God bless you.

❖

Spiritual Growth

You are all doing a certain amount of spiritual work and you are all on different steps of the ladder, which illustrates the level of your commitment. Your actions speak greater than your words; that's what it's all about. Those on the lower rungs of the ladder cannot be expected to know what those on even the next rung are pursuing. Yet those on the higher levels of attainment must bend their knee, look down and help those below them with love and compassion, as must the ones who are above them.

All must learn to give and take, to compromise and be humble. Humility is the greatest gift God has given to man. With humility you can bow with love and compassion to the very lowest without crushing them. It is still possible to cause injury due to a lack of understanding, but there is a great difference between ignorance and cruelty.

I am speaking of our brothers and sisters who scatter the seeds of love in every level of life. Those ones who have been put into the highways and byways of the Earth plane are like the good shepherds. They are given knowledge and the understanding. God brings them into the fold and fills them with thoughts, words and actions that come from a spirit of love and kindness. They then know joy and gradually learn how to balance their minds and the senses that go with it so that they can feel God's power when touching the lives of others they are serving.

The mind is the controller of everything. But so many think only with their impulses, which is the lower self — and that leads only to disaster. The mind has to open to the higher self, which will lead it with wisdom, much like pouring oil into a lamp. As it does so, the light shines through the eyes.

There are many things that have been sent into the world that humanity has no idea about and many things you do not hear about, but God works in mysterious ways in many parts of the world. The times are coming now for greater changes. People must learn to respect one another, care for one another and then God will give them purpose in life. It is a purpose that leads to serving every man and woman they meet, learning not to abuse or misuse them.

It produces a balance and a mastery of their understanding of the higher spiritual things of life, leaving space for all in which they can live and serve one another as the Master has said. I (Han Wan) am touching a lower level, as each one should give to the level below. This creates a balancing of the scales, because then you are serving at your level no matter what the deed. As you give, God gives you more strength and also the ability to more accurately serve the needs of your fellow man, because your understanding increases with service.

God will be the refuge, as He will be the strength in every need. No human soul who seeks in His holy name will ever be left wanting. When you reach to the Lord you find balance in your life and your eyes behold the light and the truth. You take in fresh energies, cosmic energies filled with divine power that the mind assimilates as a new energy and a new awareness. These energies heal and dissolve negativity. The power is so great that it dissolves negative discord and illumines the mind to a higher spirituality and reenergizes the bodies of humans.

When that happens there will be no more diseases, because the world will be purified of all its contamination. Through destructive ways of life much that is vital to life itself has been eliminated. The trees that cleanse the atmosphere and balance the oxygen levels on the planet are quickly being depleted. Your waters, your atmosphere and even your animals are being destroyed. A pattern from thousands of years ago is being repeated, when humans thought their way was the only way, and as a result brought great suffering upon themselves.

❖

Differences Between the Spirit and the Material Worlds

My world of spirit is reality and your world, the material world, is illusion, an elusive world. We can come to your world and communicate. But you can come to my world of spirit only in your sleep state, because you do not yet have the ability or the power to cross the lines into this side where it's so much more beautiful.

Yet you must come into the Earth's vibration; otherwise, it would take you eons of time to evolve. This is because the laws, different on this side, are automatic. Here there is no resistance. On the spirit plane is a great cosmic stream of energy and power, and in that stream one learns to respect and obey the automatic laws that operate there. On the planes of spirit there is an understanding of the value of those laws. But on the material plane, by using the mind as a searchlight, one must seek out what is positive from negative — which is the correct use of mind over matter.

The positive builds the power to ignite the correct use of the creative process. Then through the spiritual energy and power, the thought form or mold created from the mind manifests. In this respect the spirit plane has something in common with the material plane because the process is the same except that the manifestation is immediate on the spirit plane.

We are all brothers from ancient times, and we came into the Earth school to reincarnate and attain the wealth of wisdom and understanding of what is of value by comprehending the spirit side of life. As you submit yourself to many lives in the Earth school, all your senses develop and enter into a spiritual radiance where they become corrected and sensitive to joy and peace.

This means that you become tuned with the God power that draws higher masters from the spirit side of life. This in turn will kindle light, harmony and love in your soul so that there is a bonding between the two worlds, which registers a stronger image of goodness. As this occurs with the help of the masters, the world becomes more balanced and God will give to you the full measure of His love, and the world shall have peace and goodwill and will prosper and progress to higher levels.

Then you will not have sickness or pain in the body, but a perfect image of God. You will graduate from the Earth school into the spiritual realms with love and joy, knowing the wonderful continuity that lies ahead. Then it is for you to proceed and obey all laws that God has made through the Ten Commandments.

Obedience must come from all mankind as it is on the spiritual planes, where the laws are automatic. On the planes of spirit there are many levels, and no one can hurt or destroy another. Even on the spirit planes where the souls of animals exist, there are laws that must be obeyed, and they cannot climb out of their vibrations until they learn to obey these laws.

Sometimes souls have difficulty understanding why they are on the Earth plane, a place so full of turmoil that they wonder if there really is a heaven world (or whatever it is called by different cultures). This is because they have to learn, and they themselves chose to come into this school. They have to learn about spirituality. A soul cannot learn it in one short life; it comes back many times into the school to learn the lessons. We all did.

"But why not learn on the spirit side if it is so wonderful?" some might ask. Because it would take eons of time to evolve on the spirit side, since there are automatic laws governing every sphere. Because the soul goes through challenges on the Earth plane, it learns much faster.

It is a great achievement when you obey the laws. Because you have been given free will, you can disobey if you want. But remember that from the day you enter the Earth school you have a blueprint of your life. So when you return home to the planes of spirit you cannot say, "I did not do this or that," because you will judge yourself, knowing what actually happened, and you cannot progress until you have paid your debts.

All must balance the scales of the causes and effects they have put out; then they can go on. It is more difficult and challenging on the Earth plane, but when you finally rise above the influences of the material world and obey the spiritual laws through the exercise of your free will, you grow quickly. That is the way it is!

Remember, you go home to spirit every night and meet your master in charge over you, then you review your problems and he shows you how to deal with them the next day. This information is recorded in the subconsciousness mind for access during your waking hours. Many get confused by this information and think you have done this or that before. But it's not that; it's a flashback of what your master has given you in your sleep state on the spirit side of the school.

You were given the way to deal with a given situation. If you follow that guidance, even though it might seem like something you have done before, you will progress because you are going to do it in the correct manner. When you go into sleep state it's different from the Earth school. Your master takes you into the spiritual planes to the levels you have attained and discusses your day with you.

He goes over it all very carefully and helps you to see it in the right way. This relieves all the pressures you carried that day, so you will be different in the morning. You become more energized and relaxed and you get things clearer in your mind to begin the new day. Often you will feel, Why didn't I think that way when I was doing it yesterday? — that sort of thing. But at the time you couldn't have, and now you think of it because the new thought has been provided by your master in your sleep state.

So mankind has chosen to come to the Earth school to grow toward enlightenment. This is self-realization. You are learning to progress spiritually. The only way you can grow toward the ideals of humanitarianism is to go through the tests of the Earth school. The Master went through all the struggles of this school to show us what was possible and that we can do the same as He did.

Life's Lessons

Life is what you make it. What you sow, you reap. Every soul has a mission; you all come for a specific purpose. You are shown the path and you arrive with your own blueprint of what that path should look like if followed. You have a higher master who is dedicated to you throughout your lifetime. This master is also a source of constant inspiration for you, but if you do not heed the influence of your master, then you are not a good pupil. This causes problems as you proceed until you learn how to behave in life's school.

For example, you must learn how to give and take in a selfless manner, recognizing that you are not the only person that matters, because God looks over all people and registers the love and the light to all. But there are many who do not give and do not think with their minds. They let their emotions rule their minds, and that blocks and mars their life path. They become angry and frustrated, and this is where they have to learn to reason things out and not block the mind with the clouds of emotion. The eyes cannot behold light when the clouds are dark.

Eventually this painful process causes so much frustration that they regret their past activities when they see others progressing while they are still beating their heads against a stone wall. They wonder why. They find that their disrespect for the laws of spirit, thinking that they know better than the Almighty, has closed their minds to the truth. The mind becomes blocked with confusion and misunderstanding when the emotions take over, and they act on impulse.

When you use your emotions to think and you act through your impulses, your confusion makes you think you are correct in your actions and that you can get away with anything. So you end up doing things that are harmful to others and to yourself. However, as a result you find that you do not progress in a real sense, and you become stagnated and feel like you're in a cold draft, without respect from your fellow man and often cut off from communication and assistance from others. Eventually, this forces you to try being nice, which leads you into better balance and communication with people you come in contact with.

You begin to realize that life is give and take, so you learn to better harmonize through this understanding put into action. You find more people and things come into your vibration, which helps you to learn more of what it takes to work with the laws of spirit.

Your mind becomes open and receptive and you develop appreciation when you comprehend what it takes to mold and build a life of peace and harmony. For example, you learn that nothing comes by demanding. You have to earn things, then doors open and you touch higher masters who have authority around you. And when they see you are trying, they appreciate your desire to do things correctly and help to push you onward and upward. This way of thinking and acting honors you and moves you into higher wavelengths, which helps you to advance.

In these higher vibrations of thought you recognize the needs of others and have a deeper desire to try to help them, and this begins to create a band of good people in fellowship so that you are brothers and sisters all. And then you discuss things amongst yourselves when you have your problems and they have theirs. Through a genuine caring and sharing, definite help is rendered to each of you.

You will often say, "I never thought of the problem in that way before," and you receive assistance as you have given it. That makes the pattern or blueprint. It also provides a salve to the soul and oil for the lamp, so that there is progress and a united energy that bonds you together with light and happiness in seeing your own progress. This helps you climb the rungs of the ladder of spiritual awareness and gives you recognition and a feeling that you have earned your place in life.

Nevertheless you still have to learn the lesson of unselfishness and lose the tendency to demand what you desire. Each rung of the ladder must be climbed one at a time, made steady and balanced, then the next can be attained with certainty. These are the things that people have to learn. Then God provides more oil to that lamp, more illumination to that soul who is illustrating the Christianity of love by caring, sharing and sacrificing its own time to help its brothers and sisters.

Then the soul advances and becomes bonded with light and love, because the people it is helping to lift a little appreciate what is done for them and respect those who show them the Christian way, the way of light and love. They too learn to respect the laws of love, never abusing or misusing those who have fallen by the wayside.

God looks on the fallen and gives them oil for their lamps and also sends them a higher power. An angelic force vibrates and influences a servant of the Earth plane who has the compassion, the love and the light in their vibrations, and this influence of love helps the fallen soul to find its foothold and restore its faith.

When that happens those souls can drink from the well of the right use of the laws of love or righteousness, using the mind, influenced by spirit, not the emotions. Then with prayer, they knock on the door and it will open. When it does, this draws the true fruits of life. None need be denied if they look with the right attitude of mind. That attitude is one of respect for the laws of love, respect for those who are trying to help them and respect for what they are being told is for their own good. In this way they dissolve their negative ways and start to use their hands and minds to do something practical for others and for their own development.

Obedience to the Laws

God gives all gifts and attributes so that they can be used for a soul's own progression. There is no excuse when these talents are misused to abuse those who are more simple-minded. These are the things that have to be put into place and balanced. God keeps a record on each and everyone so that no one can say, "This is what happened, I did not do that." There is no hiding who we are and what we have done; nothing is hidden. You might try, but it doesn't work.

The Master is the light, love and compassion, and He understands all weaknesses of the flesh. But as He himself said, "Get thee behind me, Satan; thou shalt not tempt the Lord thy God." All have to respect law and order and not allow the lower self to take control and become abusive. That is the satanic vibration of mankind's lower nature.

When you allow the lower satanic vibrations to control you, it draws entities of the lower worlds who are evil, abusive and weak and who will misuse in every way. All have to learn that this is why you come into this school. This is a school of spiritual progress and you must accept the bitter cup. You have to sacrifice the lower self in the pursuit of the Father/Mother/God. As you repent and do your best to pray, asking for higher assistance, you will be delivered from all weaknesses of the flesh by your desire to overcome them and by doing good and not destroying.

What you give comes back to you. Your mind begins to change and you become more and more gentle and peaceful within, in tune with your higher self. You develop a desire for things that are peaceful to the soul, such as listening to soft, happy music that gives energy and life to your soul and mind. The mind becomes receptive to spiritual influences and you have a sense of inner happiness. You develop the habit of refreshing yourself through deep breathing, which draws cosmic energy and stirs the ethers through your body, giving you a sense of balance and a feeling that you are in charge of your own will and are becoming more and more in tune with the God-power. You become inspired to do better things, reaching up, testing new things and advancing with wisdom and understanding. That gives you peace at the end of your day and things to look back on that you have done with pride, joy and feelings of inspiration.

As you do God's holy will, helping those around you, you will be stimulated, reenergized and happy feeling the positive energies surround you. You will delight in the words of wisdom spoken and the joy given to others, seeing the light and the changes of the God-man in your communications. Then in your times of relaxation you will feel the joy of discussing many topics related to higher spiritual awareness.

Guidance

Each soul is connected to a master and learns as it goes forward that it will advance, but if it does not, they cannot push it. That would take away free will. The masters must stand back and wait for a soul to ask for assistance. *You have to ask.* Christ says, "Ask in my name and I will give unto you all things be it good for your soul." The soul evolvement is the important part, and He gives you what is best for you. This means that all requests for help might not be answered because it would not be good for you. People must learn that they cannot command, but that is what the people of your world are doing. They demand, and that's wrong. They cannot demand and abuse other souls to get what they want; that is weak and full of the ego self and not of service to their fellow man.

When using force to try and get one's demands met, whether it be with physical force or manipulation of words, there is a great price to pay. As Christ said, "Suffer the little children to come unto me and I will give them rest." He gives rest to the weary, the heavy-laden and the sorrowing, and woe be to those who abuse those who are in need. They will pay a great price. There is a time of reckoning before us. As you say, "What goes around, comes around in time." What you sow, you reap.

❖

The Value of Suffering

Sickness is good in that you learn through experiencing it. You have to go through it sometimes so you can gather knowledge and understanding of spirituality through enduring the suffering of all things for love's sake.

The Master said to learn through compassion. If you did not have any sickness, my children, you would not know what sickness was and could not identify with it. Then you would cast it aside and say, "I don't understand that."

So it has to be that each and every person must experience all examples of all vibrations of the Earth world in their spiritual evolvement. You chose to come into this Earth plane to balance and grow spiritually, and this requires that you go through different schools while you are here. Some come into the world very much evolved already, but it is their desire to return to endure a mission. They choose it for their spiritual progress.

For example, they might have returned to overcome the weaknesses of a past incarnation. Perhaps they held some hateful, angry thoughts of discrimination, and this incarnation gives them an opportunity to come back and endure certain conditions so that their minds become stronger and more pure in eliminating the darkness that had controlled it. So they go through that lifetime, and as a result they learn to see things from a different viewpoint. Their minds absorb and retain the things they have learned through these experiences, and therefore evolve and become more in harmony with the soul, which is perfect in its understanding.

The soul also has to become stronger, purer and more spiritual. This is how man evolves. Observe how the winds blow. Look at what the wind does, then prepare and protect yourself from the storms that the winds can cause. How much greater is it when the storms are within the body! No one sees what is going on inside, but the mind is holding that frustration until it can understand that the higher self helps to bring peace, pacifying and calming the winds to a gentle flow so that the mind again becomes peaceful, restored to a divine state of balance. Then the soul trusts more and advances.

Even physically deformed people learn to show respect and caring for others and forget their disabilities. Thus all suffering endured gives progress to the soul. A person might not live long, but the time is sufficient to give that person the balancing of the scales that they required. God gives them that time and then they quickly return home to the planes of spirit and move forward. There is a transformation that transfigures the body and mind, and those people might have a very peaceful time nearing the end of their Earth journey. In this way the soul is prepared for its return to the spirit plane from which it came. That is how evolution goes for everyone on the different levels.

There are seven different levels on each of the seven planes. After the seventh plane you are into that wonderful illumination, but that is a very high level. That is where we of the Great Brother/Sisterhood of Light are, and that is why we are able do our healing work amongst you, releasing much pain and discomfort and giving healing to the mind that God wishes for those souls who are not in a balanced vibration so that those who have endured much throughout their life can be helped.

It is an opportunity they have been given so that their minds become more receptive and able to think clearly again. With this healing and clearing of the mind, their faith can be restored to a positive outlook. That is evolvement, mind over matter, a return to health and trust — as the Master says, "to have faith, hope and charity." Charity/love begins at home, within the true self.

With this attitude you learn humanitarian ways where love and light are intermingled. This leads to service rendered to your fellow man no matter their color or creed. You don't think who or what they are; all you wish to know is that you can help them. This is true compassion, humanitarianism and love, love that is unconditional. God gives you the power to serve and you do not question God. You hold your faith, your trust and your obedience to His holy word.

When you come into that humility, as the Master taught humility, you have no other thought. Nothing is in your way to stop you because you have learned God's precious way to love, to respect and to always give your best. That is the way it is.

❖

The Blessing of Sacrifice

Music is a great gift from God, and there are many souls who have come into the Earth plane during a certain period to leave a legacy of that light to help humanity become a little more alert and attuned to the love of spirit. It allowed these musicians to touch a little further into the spiritual path by offering a service to the world and then returning home to the planes of spirit.

Often these souls remained unaware of their true life purpose, their blueprint, and sacrificed much of their life during their sojourn on Earth. Had they been aware of their life's pattern and escaped some of the suffering they had to endure, they might have spoiled the blueprint and not left their gift of spiritual beauty behind. But may I say that much of the music today is satanic, not music of the soul; it is just hysteria!

❖

The Mind and Its Correct Use

You have to see the good, think the good and use your mind. The mind is the motor of control and the higher self feeds the mind. You must not allow your lower self, which is the devil in man, to control the mind. The lower self is represented by the physical senses and the emotions. Typical symptoms of the lower self are anger, envy, lust and power, which are so abusive to other souls.

When people are dominated by and live from the lower self, they become egoistic and use their powers for selfish purposes, often abusing those who are weaker. That is not the God within. When people seek the vibrations of the lower self, they draw lower vibrations and lower entities found on those planes who can control them. These are departed souls and lower elements who are evil and have not progressed. They will use and abuse those who open up to their control through the misdirection of their thoughts into lower vibrations.

People do this through negative thinking and allowing their thoughts to drop out of the light through any means, whether intentional or through abusing the body and mind by, for example, taking drugs that open the door to darkness. By not taking care of yourself, being overtired or eating the wrong foods, you can pull down your energy and open the doors to darkness. When you consume your food, first bless it that it will serve to reenergize the needs of your body, then give thanks for what you have been given.

If you open your mind to negative thinking, you open the door to negative entities and their influence, to the false prophets of the inner and the outer planes. If you project your mind to positive thoughts, however, you draw the positive vibrations. When you are low you close the door to the light and draw in the darkness, attracting the wrong energies. When you are weak you must seek higher help to pull you back up into the light. Once you have learned your lesson, then you go on and teach others. You say, "This is the way; don't play with fire." People have to learn to cloak themselves in light, for light is life and God is in the light and is the light.

When people do this they learn that they should respect and obey, not abuse, the laws of love, using them in the correct way with prayer, faith and courage and knowing that God is the almighty power. Then they will be enriched, because automatically they are drawing the ethers, which are full of an energy that cannot be seen, but can be sensed and felt, much like a warm breeze. These energies are spiritually filled with a loving, caring vibration that brings peace.

Peace be still and know the I Am which is God within you. Do not search outside yourself but look

inward. There you have the portals or petals of the
lotus flower of the soul where all the energies and
many, many doors have to open. You cannot open
them all in one life because you don't have sufficient
understanding. As you evolve, you learn; and as you
learn, you will not forget but will hold that understanding forevermore. "As you sow, you reap your
reward," but the reaping, the reward, is not on the
Earth plane.

❖

Timing and Personal Evolvement

You have what we call the lamp, which is a blueprint
— that is, the blueprint of your life. You come with it
and you assemble the pieces of the plan to the best of
your ability, as it is your choice how it develops. God
has given you free will. You can make the plan work,
or you can damage it; that is your choice. As you
progress and go into that life doing the best you can,
then when you return back home to spirit, you see
what you have accomplished. This is registered in front
of you automatically, and when you have followed your
blueprint by obeying the guidance of the higher self,
that is when you experience joy. As the Master says,
"Now come with me; no, don't go that way. This is the
way you come to see the glory of God."

You are given a different robe that symbolizes your
dedication. That is your new robe to wear because
you have honored the Father/Mother/God in your life

and have given your best through your spiritual understanding. You will have great joy; it is not instilled into the soul with gold and silver, things of the material world, but with an identity that represents love, beauty and wisdom. No one can take it from you; it is infused into the soul, given by God, and no man can take away what the Lord has given. It is an automatic law that as you sow in the school of life, you reap your harvest with the fruits of your labors, with recognition through the Father/Mother/God.

As you become spiritually stronger your life becomes more progressive and your spirituality unveils more wisdom. You have joy, you radiate light and your energies are far more bountiful. Others will sense your energies. You will attract more people to you because they will sense that you have something they don't have. In this way you are able to help them open other doors of the mind that will allow them to proceed and gain more spiritual refreshment, thus making them even more inquisitive about what you are doing, such that they ask for, and you give them, more direction. This is what motivates people to knock upon the door of higher spiritual awareness. When it opens you need "to ask in the Master's name and He will give you all things that are good for your soul." But in that asking, don't intrude or push your weight around, because you will not receive that way.

God's greatest gift to mankind is humility, and those who are ready will have it. Everybody should start wherever they are to serve, to give something of themselves in dedication to their fellow man and to God, not making excuses, because that is the weakness of the flesh. Cross your bridges as you come to them; you cannot cross them before you are ready. Be cautious; if the bridge that is being prepared for your next step is not finished, then you will fall into the gully and lose a great deal.

Therefore, be patient. You must do some sowing before the reaping, before the construction of the foundation of the next step. The foundation must be strong so that you can stand on it and feel the ground under your feet before you can step forward. If you do not do this, you can be careless and overanxious, missing valuable parts and failing to put them into the structure you are building. If you jump the gun, it might be the jewel in the crown that is missing. So let go and say, "Peace be still and know the I Am which is God within." That is where the mind ends and God takes over. Then the still, small voice will tell you what to do.

You will seek by thought, tuning in to the divine power and to your higher master, who will guide you to what to do next. As you become aware of that guidance, obey it. Become a humble, obedient and patient servant of God's will, not pushing to jump into what you are not yet capable of carrying out before its time. Wait until the count is in and then you will be ready to take action. Then you gain what is to be given to you. You have to watch and pray and wait.

It is a process of gathering the tools required for the next step in your development. This means that while you gather you must pray hard, have faith and be patient, tending your garden as you wait. There is always something you can do with your energies, and then out of those energies will come a light that will be absorbed into the mind, making it receptive to receiving a greater wisdom that helps you open doors. You will be glad that you have completed what is needed in the gathering process, because then you will have the proper tools for the next step. You will be able to grow, and the seeds you plant will manifest and evolve to another level where there is more power and a greater need.

More inspiration will then be given to you physically, mentally and spiritually. Then there is a joining with other groups of like mind that are all at the same level of balance and ready to join together to increase their force far greater in number and strength. In this way it becomes possible to combat your weaknesses and gather the wisdom, understanding and foresight to help others, opening their minds to receive God's wisdom through those of you who are now into the field of service with your minds receptive, receiving the principles of what to do to serve God and mankind.

Sometimes souls have to take a rest. They might have worked hard but now must wait, watch and gather patience so that they are not overtaxed mentally or physically. The spirituality they have gained would then be in perfect attunement with the higher self, enabling them to move onto a path that will enlighten all as they perform their service to their fellow man. It means rest, peace, serenity and training the mind to have faith, control, relaxation and trust on a higher level. In this way these souls will contribute at the right times in the correct order so that there is no discord.

Handling Temptation

In the lower self is the tempter's snare. In your different levels you are tempted; therefore you have to say, "No, that is not right. Father, forgive me for my thoughts, but lead me where Thou will, so that I will obey Thy laws and Thy holy will, so that I shall not fail in my mission this time and so that I will climb the rungs upward and my goals will be in balance. May I be a humanitarian, loving my neighbor as myself, sharing, caring and helping the poor, the heavy-laden, the sick and the downtrodden. May I be given that understanding and the strength to fight the good fight where love and might are one with the Father and my soul. May my soul be intact, not in parts or pieces of negative greed and selfishness. May I be given the strength to cope and fight a good fight with love and light and humility."

Those are the important issues, and when you live

that way there is no test you can fail. But when you fail to live this way you have guilt and anger and a "poor me" attitude, saying to yourself, "Why should I have to suffer?" You become angry and abuse others on the "right path," wishing to be where they are — but that is not possible when you misuse and abuse your fellow man. You have to straighten the path, to put back what you have abused and let it go. Reach up and put your thoughts into the right sector and ask the Master to help you, repenting your ways and asking for forgiveness, acknowledging that you are ready to do whatever spirit asks of you that will put you back into the stream of energy and harmony.

You have to work it out, but once you get into the right field of service you will be happy within yourself and you will have others around you who are also happy as you unite in a bond of light and love again. In this way you progress, not allowing your thoughts and actions to fall back into another negative field of desire. You might need to learn some of your lessons the hard way, but in the end it pays off as you pass your tests for the master.

❖

Service

You must first love yourself, then love all as you love yourself. It is simple, because if you don't love yourself you will only have envy. In this way you heal yourself of your guilt, accepting your true spiritual identity while serving with humility, love and a sincere attitude of caring. When you give out love, you receive it back.

God feeds the hands that feed others. So give as generously as you can, working beside others when they have a little difficulty. Share, care and show others how to rise above their obstacles, helping them to keep their balance. That is one hand helping the other. As you give unto others, so will it come back to you. Everything is registered on your blueprint, every thought, every deed you do. You cannot hide the truth of what you have done. Actions speak greater than words, so when the thoughts and words do not match the actions, pray and ask for help, and in asking you will receive. The thoughts must be pure for the action to have real value.

Dealing with Fear

Don't carry fear. Pray every day that God will bless your home, that it will be protected from all the dangers of the outside world. Ask it in His holy name. Ask that the Master will lead you where He will, that you will have a safe vibration around you and that whatever has to be will be, but that you have your security. Don't carry negative vibrations. Don't think about it, because you can do nothing at this point in time. When your mind is inspired by the higher self's stirring certain ideas within you such as, "I should be doing *this*," then it would be good to pay attention to that and act on it.

If the higher self is telling you something, it is likely that an event is coming close, so act upon that inspiration. There will be no regrets and you will not be found wanting; it is better to be safe than sorry. God does give guidance to those who are in tune with their higher self. Those who are in constant communion through the day are led, because they are connected to the masters on the higher levels who are God's masters to the world. This is what is meant by the statement to "pray without ceasing." In this way you are in tune with your higher self and in harmony with the soul.

The soul is the almighty power within you, and God registers to that power within the soul. Those who have locked the doors are aimlessly wandering because they know not what they do and are like a leaf in the wind.

The Levels of Spiritual Growth

There are many different spheres in which we progress, and in every plane there are also seven different levels. You reach these higher levels through different incarnations and are given free will while you are in the school of life. In this way you make or mar your progress. Those who dedicate themselves to this evolution will know joy, for they will know their

Father/Mother/God, Who gives pure light and love. This dedication also requires that you respect your body, not abusing it but using it for the good of mankind.

In your spiritual growth you will have a peace which passeth all understanding. You are enriched in mind, in body and in soul. There are many vaults and many, many levels of consciousness and higher spirituality. At each successive level you become more and more in tune with spirit. When you have fulfilled your mission you are initiated into another level and receive another standard, a symbol representing your work on the spiritual plane that allows you to be a servant in one of the planes equivalent to the level you have reached. There you will again progress spiritually with love and dedication to those you are amongst, those who need help, care, teaching and comforting.

You go through schooling on the Earth plane until you achieve a level of consciousness and understanding wherein you no longer have to go back to the Earth plane unless you are sent by God on a special mission to be a pillar of light for a greater cause. Then the light will be given with the wisdom needed for those who are seeking greater understanding.

❖

Communication with Higher Guidance

To live and remain in the light each day, you need to concentrate on the work, meaning your service.

You have a higher master, an instructor overshadowing you at all times, just as your guardian angel is always there. They protect you and vibrate with you, keeping your mind operating correctly and in balance as you obey God's guidance.

Through your intuition your master gives you the wisdom to impart and the actions to fulfill, creating and manifesting according to God's will so that you can proceed forward in the light. That is how the mind operates correctly, and as you progress you gather in knowledge and understanding.

As you are going forward, don't let your mind go this way and that way. Keep your concentration on what you are doing. Your work, no matter what it is, is important, so you need to be involved and do that work to the best of your ability during your hours of service. When you put out your prayer in the morning before you begin your day, that prayer takes you through your day and is registered to the higher self. God cares for and protects you, and your master who is with you is dedicated to your life from the beginning to the end of your life journey. You are never alone.

As you ask each day, it is registered. Then when you have your little break for food, digest the food you take and say, "Thank you, Father, for this food. May it be blessed and energized for the needs of my body. I thank you, Father, for all blessings from above. May your angels watch over me and may I be inspired, may

I complete my day successfully. May I be cloaked in light and protected from all dangers that I do not see, and may I return to my home in safekeeping under your care. Thank you, Father, and bless all who are within this building that they too may be cared for and protected. Just as I seek for myself I ask for all. Thank you, Father, Thy will be done."

There are no ifs, ands or buts — it is in perfect harmony. So don't put out your prayers and then question them afterward; that is no good. You have no faith if you do that; you are breaking the stream of creative energy. People have to learn not to be airy-fairy. You have got to be in perfect harmony with the challenge, true to yourself, have dignity, strength, faith and courage to commit yourself to the one God and all the power He holds. His will will be done, and no one can take away what is yours. Give your trust to the divine power as you pour out your energies in the right flow of the cosmic stream of love and light.

❖

Creating Correctly

You have to be strong in your faith and not stumble, knowing that God's will will be done. Ask God's power to be with you. Ask that you will be inspired by the Holy Spirit and that a higher master will always guide you, helping you to master each situation. If you think with the ego and let the lower self take over, you are drawing a different concept of energy that is aggressive and abusive and that uses others with words — cloudy words that have no substance and blow with the wind.

That is characteristic of the false prophet who cannot find true spirituality. Their downfall is that they do not listen to the higher self, and God will not allow His masters to be used and abused in circumstances that are not of the light. So without the higher power, sooner or later these souls fail in their undertakings and they bring everything and everyone attached to themselves down with them.

Because they are full of self and words without action, they are living with a constant mist of clouded thoughts. They become disillusioned, bitter and angry and can only be destructive because evil, lower energies come, using them for abusive things to destroy the good. There is much evil today in the world because mankind has fallen from its pedestal of light and has disrespected God the Father and His Son, Jesus Christ.

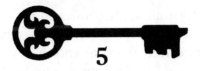

Reincarnation and Karma

Guidelines of the School of Life

As I look upon the energies today, reviewing all countries of the world and deciphering the energies of the material, mental and spiritual vibrations, I see humanity's mind filled with much disturbance. It is sad to see the world in the closing vibrations of this era immersed in clouds of darkness instead of light and harmony. Many souls on the spirit plane are saddened by what they find.

People have to learn to repent their ways and come back to God the Father and obey His laws. Humanity cannot live without the Father and the Son, Jesus the Christ, Who is the love of the Father. He is the heart of God made manifest in the image of mankind so that mankind would know and understand that life is a continuity that allows it to climb the rungs of the ladder of spiritual energy and awareness.

However, to do this souls must come again and

again; therefore, all souls come and go on the Earth plane many times. This is called reincarnation. It is not possible to feed the soul with all experiences in one short span of life. Humanity must understand the philosophies of the soul. The soul needs love, wisdom and spiritual understanding through serving its fellow man, treating one another with respect and love and living a life filled with sharing and caring. In this way God is in the hearts of all and there is unison and peace. The mind then absorbs the peace into the soul where love stimulates it more and more.

Before coming, you chose your parents. You are born into a country that will represent your identity for that particular incarnation. Before you leave the spiritual plane you are put into what you might call a cocoon of light, and although you have a mind, your soul is put into a state of sleep. You thereby lose the awareness you have been vibrating in during a spiritual state of consciousness on the other side. Once you are ready to come into the Earth plane, you must wait for the parents you have chosen according to the genes required for your evolvement.

If a soul is an old soul — that is, one with a considerable spiritual evolvement — it might wait quite a long time before returning to the physical plane. Your consciousness is in the seed of your future body at conception. During the pregnancy you have a guardian angel who is dedicated to you and continues with you after the birth process and until your transition back to spirit. That is the duty these angels have taken on, and it is also their job to watch over the physical body and to inspire you to a certain extent.

Once you are born into the Earth plane, it takes some time to become aware of all your energies. No matter what your state, whether you have the care of two parents, one parent or none at all, you are always under the care and love of God's embrace. No matter what condition you are living under, you are always overshadowed by His love.

When you come into your incarnation you come with a blueprint, which is also in God's care. As a part of that blueprint there is a time of arrival into the Earth plane and a time of departure or transition. In other words, there are no such things as accidents. The time of departure was predestined from the beginning.

Some have to pay karmic debts through their physical bodies. The subject of karma and the sicknesses that can fall upon the physical body and the mind is a very deep question.

In addition to your guardian angel who watches over you, you also have a high master who is taught and trained before your incarnation in preparation for it. They too are going through their evolvement while they are with you. In other words, your growth contributes to their growth.

During your infancy there is a great deal of work in feeding the nerve centers as well as the cells of the body. The mind needs loving care. The creative aspect of the soul's advancement is greatly influenced by the love it absorbs, the strength the mind receives and what goes into the body in the infant vibrations of the mind. This is not an easy process, and many children have a great deal of disharmony in their infancy.

For example, the mother can affect the child by not respecting her own body during her pregnancy. She might abuse it by what she takes internally, and this causes suffering to the infant. Although this is part of experience, these conditions can be surmounted as the soul gets into its first seven years. This is a period of making or breaking the mold for the rest of the soul's life.

During this time it needs love, care and sharing; it also needs discipline and routine. Routine is very important; without it a soul becomes lawless and undisciplined. Routine creates a sense of mind over matter and a respect for time.

Now, in the soul's blueprint there are what you could call many holes in the pattern that can be destructive unless there is discipline. This is because within the framework of a soul's destiny, it has free will, and without discipline a soul would abuse others in the pursuit of its own selfish ends, including an open disregard for its parents.

At the age of seven the roots begin to take hold; the mind reaches out and begins to seek further incentive. Hopefully, the child is educated and taught to read and write, to put its feet on the ground and learn. All souls come into the Earth plane with certain attributes that help form their daily life. After another seven years, at age fourteen, a soul might begin to get a little out of line, which comes through emotions and frustrations. At this stage it is neither child nor adult.

As the soul proceeds to the third stage of life, age twenty-one, it settles down and absorbs more. It is then easier for the higher master assigned to it to enlighten its mind. During this entire twenty-one-year growth period the higher self, the spiritual ego, is in charge. After that period when the soul has attained maturity, it is spiritually responsible for all its actions. It cannot at that point blame others. Until the age of twenty-one it is not held completely responsible for all the things it does because it is not yet truly balanced.

It takes many years and many incarnations to complete the soul's evolution and come to a level where there is respect and dignity. On the Earth plane the karmic debts are paid; however, those who repent what they have done are given a light that helps them, and life continues onward and upward on the seven planes.

❖

Your Soul's Earth Vehicle

When this Earth life is finished, some do not understand what has happened to them. "Where do we go?" they ask. Many do not think there is a heaven, but think this is the only life. It is sad to think that humans are not aware of the evolution of the soul and do not know they have had many incarnations or that they will return after a time to continue their spiritual education in the school of life.

Many do not know it is their choice to come back to learn specific things for the betterment of their growth. God provides that time and gives them a physical vehicle or body. When you choose to come back, you also choose your parents so that they can provide the appropriate physical sheath or outer coat for that incarnation; the rest is spiritual, ethereal. The spirit body is spirit and the ethereal bodies are the the finer bodies. They are intermeshed and put into the physical sheath, the cloak that covers your true identity during your sojourn in the school.

The aura is the spiritual energy that surrounds the body. The auras of some souls are more beautiful because they are greater servants. As you progress the aura becomes more and more illumined — that is, of the spirit, but it is actually the energies of spirit. Your spirit body has cloaks, thus you have the aura, which surrounds the body and indicates the level of attainment of your spirituality.

Balancing the Scales

Sometimes when a soul chooses its parents it also chooses to be born into a body that is deformed. That too has a purpose. It could be a karmic condition the soul wants to experience, enduring it for love's sake. As it does the best it can, there is a potential to progress spiritually and become a better person.

For example, the soul could be trying to learn patience and tolerance toward people around it, and as it moves forward it acquires understanding. Also, there could be some people around that soul who are connected to that karmic condition who are also helping. That is part of their contribution. This could be members of the soul's family, and that might be why they were chosen by the soul who chose the deformed body. They all can learn a great deal from the association with that soul.

But if they abuse that soul and let it suffer more than the disabled soul is already enduring, then they are failing in their task of giving service of their time and compassion. In that case they have failed to pass the test they owed from a previous time.

Each soul has a blueprint for its life pattern. Some souls might have a so-called accident, but everything is on a schedule. That imprint on a soul's path is exclusively its own. It learns from every experience. It is in God's book, and it knew before it touched the Earth — because each thing was shown to it — what its life would be and what it could do.

Because you have free will, you can choose to take a different path, and any different choices you make will be automatically done. But if you go against the guidance of your higher masters, then you must take the consequences.

Accidents also happen due to carelessness or abuse of some kind. The soul has to endure that disability for a time, and through it is another opportunity to learn. It might repent the error of its ways and learn how to deal with it. In this case the accident did not have to occur, and a lot of suffering was unnecessary.

❖

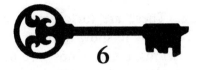

6

What Comes After Death

Life Continues

After your soul leaves the body of flesh behind, you are taken to the light and ascend into the planes of spirit. Here the guardian angels take you. When you wake up on the other side you find that you are no longer in the school of life but in a rest home where you are cared for for a time. Life begins anew, but you have to do as you are told.

You have to learn to obey the laws, which are automatic laws where no one can hurt another. You learn that there are different spiritual planes and many levels on each plane. And you learn that that is the true world of reality and that all have eternal life.

Everything you have in your world, we have in perfectness. And as you grow in spirituality you gather much more harmony and beauty because God is the beauty of harmony. There are masters who teach in the halls of learning, the halls of music and the halls of philosophy. These are for all who are ready to receive, but they have to show respect.

As your consciousness develops, you become more and more spiritual and aware. When everyone learns to obey the laws, then nothing gets out of line. You sense that there is peace when one obeys the ultimate laws. Also, you meet departed loved ones. You might not be on the same level as they are, but they can come down to you if you are not as high as they are. To visit them you would have to have your energies revved up to their vibration. That is how it works.

Everything is through automatic laws, and higher masters send those who see to all these things. They are the ones who help those who seek their loved ones.

The Book of God

The akashic record is where every person's identity resides, and only God and the angel of transition have the keys. No one can interfere or see into it, as it is under God's divine power. Every soul is prepared for transition; it is not like the snap of a finger. You speak of accidents, but there is no such thing as an accident. The time of transition is predestined. The departure is prepared for each individual.

Each individual comes with an ideal life pattern printed on their blueprint. You can make or mar this pattern, as mankind has free will. But before you come you are aware of the duties you are coming to perform and the lessons you want to learn. This school is for the soul's advancement, not just for a few years of personal enjoyment.

Life is a mission that involves lessons so that you can evolve. If you choose, when you come to the Earth school to take the easy way, the path of selfishness, then look out, because you will surely find disillusionment and disappointment when you see the record of what you have done when you go back to your true home after your transition from the Earth school. Then you will regret things you should have done differently and you will say, "I have to go back and do that all over again in another life."

That is the way it goes; you have free will to make or mar your life pattern or blueprint. There is a life pattern which some people think of as fate, but there is also free will within the boundaries of that life pattern, and it is very important for people to know that.

If you have purity in your life, you can look at your life record while you are still in the Earth school. Some souls who have progressed far enough can review the akashic record in more detail, but no one can change the akashic record; it is in God's hands The soul must have purity before it can view the record, because if the purity were not present, some souls might have a tendency to elaborate on what they saw and fantasize, which would cause more disruption than good results. It is more important to look at the spirit behind the phenomena.

❖

Suicide

Taking one's life is wrong; it is due to a mental sickness. It comes to pass from a world filled with stress and with situations that some people cannot tolerate, so they seek to end their suffering. Their minds are like blackened pots whose energies have been out of alignment, making their thoughts fearful, creating mountains out of molehills, blowing little things way out of proportion. Because of the great fear and confusion, their minds are constantly in a jumble, which they just cannot stand. So they feel their only option is to get away from it all by taking their own life.

When this happens the soul is not in its true light, so there is forgiveness. There are helpers who work with these souls. For example, they are taught a spiritual discipline. They are taken to the pools of healing and their minds are relieved of all anxieties and frustrations. There are physicians, spiritual healers who look upon them and release all the confusion and blocks they might have had for many years.

Comas

Persons who go into a coma are still under the care of divine power and might be out of the body in a transient state. They could be doing something for their own good; they know they are under good guidance and they are given peace of mind and soul. When it is complete, their higher master influences them to return their consciousness to their body, but during their absence they have been reenergized. When they wake up it's as if they had been in a dream.

Different Levels

In each plane there are several levels, and you can go from one level to another. There is a master who is in charge of each level. If you wished to meet and greet a loved one who is on a higher level than your own, you must be cloaked and energized. You are taken by a higher master when this is permitted, and you can stay only a short time because the protective energies will not hold. This is how you distinguish the levels of evolution of a soul.

Those on a higher level can visit a lower level, and they too must be cloaked in a protective vibration to descend to those levels. Then it is possible for them to give incentive and enlightenment to those who have not gone quite so far.

There are many different halls of learning and healing governed by higher masters who are in charge of every plane. For example, I (Han Wan) have a temple where I teach. Many come during the sleep state from your Earth plane into my temple of light to learn. They are taught wisdom to bring back into the Earth plane to share with others. They share the love and the brotherhood of man no matter the color, and are taught that there is only one Father/Mother God, almighty, all-powerful, loving and caring, the creator of all life. This is very important for people to understand at this critical time.

The Bridge of Light

The Master is much in your world today, looking over all in your world. He is helping many who have been abused and misused and those who die. He and his ambassadors of light are making bridges of light to take these souls into the spiritual plane, to the astral plane, so that they can be comforted. For they know not where they are because they have not been released out of their bodies in the right way; instead they have been blasted out of their bodies through man's use of evil, destructive weapons. Many thousands are in a state of confusion, so they are being cared for, relieved of their traumas and given serenity and peace with God's love. This is what we are having to handle on the spiritual side at this time.

The Father is loving and caring, and His energies flow to every level of power on the spiritual planes. There is eternal light, and no pain or sorrow. Love emanates through every sphere, and all know spiritual peace and relaxation in music out of your understanding, because it is far more beautiful. All that you have on the Earth plane, we have in a greater degree, far more beautiful in its perfection.

Nothing is destroyed or dies here. The animals

have their kingdom, too; they have their place and have no fear. The spirit world operates through automatic laws, and no one can alter those laws to hurt or destroy life; they have not that power. Thoughts are living things and no one can go against God's law. We have beautiful flowers not of your world and we have healing streams and pools.

Those who have had much sickness in their Earth life are taken to rest homes where they are cared for and their minds erased of all the traumas and the sufferings they have endured. They have no pain and their minds are released of their burdens. Their spiritual body is then reenergized and they are overjoyed when loved ones they have known come to greet them. There are beautiful gardens and halls of music where they can replenish lost energies and gain peace and serenity. There are also temples of wisdom where there is much to be learned.

We too have our sacred places, far greater than your world. But I do not come down the great stairway to overpower your minds with more than you can absorb at one time. I feel it is good that the blessings are given in God's way as He embraces you all in His love, with the peace which passeth all understanding.

The mind is the motor that holds the good energies. May the mind be ever crystal clear in the purity of thought. From the mind come the words, but words are nothing without actions; actions speak greater than words. It is actions *with* words that you need to give, with spirituality and with respect for everything. You need to look upon all your brothers and sisters with love and light, giving them a boost and comforting them when they are low in spirit, putting them back on their way onward and upward.

When you give a boost to their morale, it helps them to once more project positive thinking and allow them to drink from the living streams of energy, which will be assimilated and stimulate their ability to control their mind. This will help them to recognize again the importance of the mission before them that has to be accomplished.

7

Prayer and Meditation

Connecting to Spirit Through Meditation

God bless you, my brothers and sisters, in all that you are endeavoring to accomplish for the good of mankind. May God give you light, wisdom and understanding. God bless you.

Learn to create in the mind a garden of color with flowers. Flowers emanate a spiritual radiation that is given to mankind. They put out a refreshing energy. You might add a few trees to your garden of the mind that will also vitalize the atmosphere around you. Then create a path leading to a little bridge running over a small stream of water so that you can walk through your garden and see its beauty. You want to be in tune with your higher self. This is the symbolism of the spirit world and all its emanation of color, God's reward of love and light.

As you create your garden you will add to it as you grow in the fields of spirit and in spiritual awareness.

Then your master, one of God's chosen servants who overshadows you throughout your life, will give to you through your intuition the illumination of wisdom to endow you with his love.

You will receive a rainbow of color that goes through your aura and strengthens your mind, giving it a motivation that helps to build faith and daily inspiration so that you don't become a closed door. Your door is open and you see the light, which gives you hope and a faith that endures all things through love, divine love. God is your refuge and you will become closer to Him because you will feel that radiation. Then the Master will register His light. It will shine through the door of the mind and stir the cosmic energies so that you can understand and become more and more intuitive to His holy will.

You will learn to listen to that inner voice that will record messages to you. You will absorb them and they will give you strength for the day, motivating a desire to dig with a silver tool into the inner portals of your being. You will unravel many mysteries and become stronger; you will have attributes that will become more and more constructive; and you will then show mankind the way. As this occurs you have a sense of knowing that what you are doing is given from a higher power, the God force, the Almighty.

Then in your sleep state you will be given your graduation. You touch into higher levels of spirituality, and as you reach out each day into your garden of the mind you find a knowledge, an understanding, that is the fruit of your labors. You will find that people you have known for a long time will look upon you with awe, saying, "How do you know these things? How have you gathered this understanding? I don't know these things." You are still the same being, the same loving, caring person, but your energies have become and continue to become stronger and more illumined.

But God keeps you in a state of humility and balance. Your senses change and your body connects to other energies. It feels as if you are cleansing the flesh that is the outer coat surrounding the real you. Then God puts a shield over you to protect you, because you are becoming more and more sensitive to the spiritual things.

God cares for all His servants who are dedicated to the cause, just as Christ taught His disciples, "Fear not the way; I am the way and the light and the truth, and as you follow in my footsteps I will give unto you all things that are good." That is the first concept.

To connect to spirit through meditation, one has to empty the mind of all heavy vibrations and then relax every nerve center and muscle. It is best not to sit in a chair that is too soft. Sit with the back straight so that you are erect and not slouched. Breathe deeply in and out, releasing all the pressures and stresses of the day. Sometimes it is good to play very soft music in the background that allows you to let go and allow peace and serenity to come over you. Any of the great musicians will do; this is very helpful in releasing stress and tension. Music is color energy and spiritual energy.

Then go into your garden and pray, saying, "Father, come into my garden that I may be with Thee and Thee with me. Heal my mind of all stresses that I may become an instrument of light and love to pour out to my fellow man. Help me to be a servant to all, caring and sharing what You give unto me.

"Father, set me free of all weaknesses of the flesh that I might be a humble, obedient servant to serve Thee in mind, in body and in spirit so that I be brought into the light. And may You send another master to watch over me so that I do not fall by the wayside. Cloak me in light, Father, as I do my humble best to listen to my inner voice. And may the Master always be my guide. May my prayers be heard and may they be answered to my understanding.

"Father, I will do my best also to serve my fellow man no matter what color or creed they be, for Thou art the only God almighty, all-powerful, Who knoweth all things and gives to all Thy children that we may gather the knowledge, wisdom, patience, love and light and learn to obey Your laws and honor them.

"As spirits clothed in a material body, this is the school You have sent us into to learn our lessons, then to graduate back to the spiritual plane, to evolve. But again we must come back into the school to evolve and become closer to thee in consciousness and purification. Grant me the grace that I might never lose the humility to love all my sisters and brothers who come before me and always share and care and do thy will.

"May I be Thy obedient servant to do Thy holy will and to be aware that Thou art with me. May Thy rod and Thy staff comfort me. May the Master register His light on my path that I may not stumble but be shown the way, and may the light draw me forward, upward and onward until I can sense the mission that You have sent me to complete. And may I always obey Thy holy word. Keep me in the light, and may the rays of the inner sun shine upon me and mine.

"Father I give unto You now the full praise, the honor and the glory for all that is given through love."

❖

Beginning Your Day with Prayer

Learn to relax and use prayer as your mantra. When you pray, ask for divine guidance every morning before you begin your day and ask for peace and goodwill to all mankind and to all life. Then you might ask that your higher master overshadow and inspire you and that you do your best to carry out your work vibration to the best of your understanding and to be guided and cloaked in the white coat of light, for that is your protection from all dangers from the outside world.

Then hold those thought vibrations during the day so that when you seek good, you draw good to yourself. Negative thoughts draw more negativity and confusion, so it is mind over matter, mind control. When you do that, you absorb the correct ethers and become more spiritually conscious. It becomes a natural thing, a daily habit like eating a meal. You know that you have a time for your meals; so also do you need a time for your prayers, which is a time for your intercession with God. Respect that time.

As a result you absorb spiritual energies that nothing can take away from you, and as you do so you progress. Your mind becomes lighter, you become a creator with greater ideas. Power flows to you with a new understanding of what we call an inceptive vibration that then allows you to give out wisdom, power and understanding. Then your vibrations will draw people to you because they sense that you have a secret energy, and this motivates other minds to communicate with you in harmony. In this way you are reaching out into the stream of cosmic energies; nevertheless, your mind can only touch what it can digest and absorb. So when you are serving others you must reach them at the level where their minds can digest and absorb what you are offering them. Then they want more and will gather more as they expand their knowledge and understanding. With their minds open there is greater advancement, because they are opening the inner portals that have been closed.

To begin your day with balance and harmony when you awake in the morning, say, "Thank you, Father, for this day and for the opportunities that are mine. May I have a good day and may my work and my place of work be blessed, together with all my colleagues. May I be in tune with my higher self, in tune with my master, and may I serve to the best of my ability. But should I have to face unforeseen circumstances, may a higher master overshadow me and give me the wisdom and the words to speak that will be beneficial to the condition.

"I ask that there will be a balance in my day and that things be worked out to my understanding and to that of my colleagues. May there be a light that will shine to bring understanding and peace and a certainty behind the cause of every situation. May I return to my home at the end of my day in safekeeping. May my home be blessed and may my loved ones who are near and dear to me have a good day. May all blessings be to Thy holy name and may a higher master overshadow me throughout my day. Amen."

People sometimes feel that their prayers are not answered, often because they are not praying in the right way. Sometimes they are not serious about their prayer; there is no sincerity, just repetition of words. When you pray for others you can make a real difference if there is sincerity in your heart.

❖

Prayer and Your Higher Master

Each soul is overshadowed by its own master, who is dedicated to that soul. But the soul must be in tune with its master. To do this you pray and ask for communication with your higher master. Say, "Dear Father God, may my master overshadow me and may he guide me, inspire me and take me over my hurdles at this time, setting me down again upon my path so that I might be put back into the driver's seat so I can face my tomorrows with a strength and reenergized vitality, using mind over matter. May I be held in the cloak of energy and power. Take me and show me the way, Father; send me on my way that I may continue to be a dedicated faithful servant to Thee and Thine. And may the Master also vibrate His light upon me to give me that extra boost to my morale that I always be upon the true pathway and shall not fail in my accomplishments. For His namesake. Amen."

If you decide to go your own way, then your master cannot intervene, as God gave you the gift of free will to make or mar your life pattern. That is what the school is all about. Nevertheless, help is always available to you. Ask and ye shall receive; as the Master said, "Knock on the door and it will open unto you. Ask in my name and ye shall receive all things be they good for your soul and its advancement." You will receive what is good for the soul's development at the right timing, because if you received all your prayers when you asked for them, you might receive things detrimental to your evolvement.

Ending Your Day with Prayer

At the end of your day before you close your eyes in sleep, meditate by going into the silence and doing your deep breathing, releasing all frustrations of the day. If you have had a bad experience and lost your temper, say, "Father, I come before You now to unveil and unravel my emotions. I ask Thy forgiveness for losing my temper, for I know better now. I also ask a blessing on the ones I allowed my anger to spill upon; may they also forgive me as I ask a blessing on them. May there be a healing and a clearance of all harmful thoughts and words spoken. May they be blessed and may their minds be relieved as I ask you to clear and cleanse my mind from all weaknesses.

"Father, may this night I meet with loved ones departed. May my home be blessed and all who are within, and may it be held in security in the hours of sleep. Father, may I be also able to go forward on the spiritual planes and be taught the ancient wisdom in my sleep hours. When I am out of the physical body and onto a higher level may a higher master take me and teach me so that when I return into my physical body to a new day it will be with a new inspiration and with the aspiration to love, to care, to share and to give out that love.

"May I then embrace all beings with the light of the Master, sharing my knowledge and understanding so that they too will behold the light and the truth. And may they learn the spiritual way of living to embrace a humanitarian attitude so that the effect of this cause brings harmony and security and so that we all make our foundations on a solid rock, knowing that Thou art that rock and that Your energies overshadow us.

"Bless all the sick and the needy, retarded, mentally sick and those who have pain, suffering and sickness of the body. Father, may they be blessed also who have no one to pray for them. May they be embraced in Thy love and care, and may Thy angels watch over them and all children who are abused and misused. May they be protected by Thy ministering angel forces along with all children in sickness of body and mind. God bless them, too. Give them strength and the power to surmount their obstacles and give unto them healing, faith and courage.

"Bless all in their different states of life, all physicians, doctors and nurses who are dedicated to serve in a humanitarian way, who give their time and their lives in dedication to the needs of the sick and the oppressed. May they be also blessed by that Holy Spirit. May Thy will always be upon my will that I shall not walk alone but hand in hand with Thee and the higher master overshadowing my day to the end of the day. I give thanks to Thee and Thy holy name, and may I return to my sleep hours to be with Thee and

Thine and to touch the halls of wisdom that I may be taught greater things and return to another day refreshed and inspired."

God bless you all. I leave you again under the radiance of the six-pointed star, the Star of David and of the Great Brotherhood of Light, of which I am that humble master. May their light so shine upon you and yours and may you walk in love, peace, health and progress every step that you climb so that you receive security in God's love. And may the Father/Mother/God embrace all in His love and light, and may Mother Mary also generate her energies to all who read the wisdom that has been here imparted.

8

The Master Jesus

Introducing the Master Jesus

Greetings to you, my brothers and sisters. As I come down the great stairway I cloak you in all energy and power and I give you the tidings of light, joy, peace and goodwill. I bring to you the essence of the Easter time, which is the time of opening the sails of the mind and the body to be purified, sanctified and blessed. At this time you regain the great spiritual mediator, Jesus the Christ.

His light and His power come into your temple to reenergize your bodies and give His blessings. As He meets you He greets you with wisdom and understanding, that you may follow in His footsteps and sow good seed that would bear good fruit in the tomorrows.

This is a time when the Master, the Christ, registers His power to the world, bringing to mind the great sacrifice He gave so that mankind would learn to love brother as self, not destroying but respecting one another. The Master is shedding His light to the world, now showing that His sacrifice was not in vain but illustrating that he who gives his life for his fellowman shall not perish but will know everlasting life. He shall find his true life and he will know the joy of a wonderful spiritual continuity.

❖

The Master Speaks

Peace be unto you. I come down to give you my blessing. May my light that is eternal shine through every page of truth that has been given. I feel that it is important that mankind shall come to terms with life and know it is part of everything, that no one is whole unto themselves. It is how you distribute and how you absorb the cosmic power which is God energy, not seen but felt. This is how I also manifest to those who are susceptible to my will and my presence.

I wish you all the blessings from the Father/Mother God and of Mother Mary, who is manifesting often in parts of your world today. I too am in your world now, but I have many cloaks, and it is not my time to show my true identity, only to certain ones of God's unit sent to parts of the world to radiate inborn love and compassion, not hate nor ego but humility. This I give unto this book that reveals many parts of world history yet to come.

I bless you, and may the lambs and the sheep have

their place. One day I shall come, and I will count them and I will put my shepherds out to the highways and byways and gather them back into the fold of light, love, peace and goodwill to all mankind. For ye are my lambs and sheep. And there will be no color bar, there will be no hate; only love and light shall shine through their souls, and their minds will be opened and set to the Father's will.

I and the Father are one in unison to all power that unites mankind who come to that state of well-being and to a higher state of consciousness that can respect the laws.

One day I will bring back the scrolls and mankind will bow in humility before me. They will be brothers all in love, peace and goodwill. That time is the new Aquarian Age. It is in its infancy now, but the times are ripening for the Father to register the power of the Holy Spirit into one great united force that will gravitate the light and encircle the world, taking it out of its bondage of hate to love, honoring and obeying the spiritual laws.

Then will mankind know no evil and will feel no pain; bodies shall again be brought into harmony and all disease will be eliminated. It will be one family united with the Father/Mother God. I will be again the shepherd amongst them for a time until they have found their balance and their way to a new age and way of life to research, not outwardly but inwardly, where the great wisdom lies in the vaults of the soul.

Then mankind shall bear no evil but only humility, joy and love; and the light shall then not be dimmed but illumined with respect. The minds of mankind shall look upon brother as equal, not looking for the bad spots. Mankind will come to be bonded in love, peace and harmony for a prosperous life. There will be a thousand years of peace without wars, and all countries will be brought into at-one-ment to share and care for one another. No one will go without.

Mankind will progress spiritually with spiritual awareness, and certain psychic abilities will permeate his whole mind in harmony. That is my blessing to your world. Until I come may it feed you and give you all peace, faith and hope for a new day and a new beginning under God's supreme power.

I and the Father are one. Were it not so I would tell you. I give this in serenity and with my soul love. May the six points of the Star of David unite every corner of the world in the united body of love, peace and tranquillity to all ages and all colors and all creeds. There is only one God who is almighty and powerful, yet wonderful, loving and caring. May that peace now be to all who shall read this book. God's blessing and my imprint shall be upon it . I bless you and yours. I will touch again. God bless you.

❖

Personal Testimonials by Some Who Have Known Edith Bruce

As a Command Officer in the Scottish Police Service I have been present on notable occasions when Edith Bruce has provided a resolution to circumstances which might otherwise have been left unanswered. I have known Edith for thirty-two years and can, without fear of contradiction, observe that her gifts are remarkable and lie outside the realms of normal understanding. However, they can relate to direct earthly matters, and the following two circumstances will illustrate the relationship with real life events.

As a young Detective Sergeant, I was working on a murder enquiry where a youth had been attacked and killed in a quarry filled with water. Leads were few so I consulted Edith, giving her the outline of what had happened. She responded by naming a district where the individual who had committed the crime lived, described the house in which he lived, including specific ornaments in the front garden, and said that clothes wet with the quarry water would be found in a chest of drawers in the individual's room.

Armed with this information, I was able to narrow

my search to a particular housing area, and within a short time found the man in exactly the place and circumstances Edith had described.

On another occasion two men had gone fishing in a small cabin cruiser on a Scottish loch. The weather became poor and the boat sank. Despite searches involving divers from the Royal Navy and the use of up-to-date technology, no trace of the vessel was found.

I consulted Edith, who had no prior knowledge of the event. She described the loch in question in specific detail and the precise place where the boat and bodies would be found.

The morning after seeing Edith, without revealing my source, I suggested that we try one last location. A diver entered the water and within two minutes found the boat and victims. This allowed loved ones some degree of peace of mind.

> — *A Command Officer in the Scottish*
> *Police Service (Anonymous)*

I first met Edith on April 20, 1976, when she was visiting with her daughter in Toronto, Canada. She was referred to me by the secretary of a well-known international motivational speaker. He had been her student for a number of years, and much of his work was inspired by the guidance he had received through Edith. Although I had been studying spiritual matters for some years, I was struck by the outstanding authority the master Han Wan displayed during the life and advisory reading I received. Something within me was deeply moved, and from that day on Edith became my primary source of solid spiritual guidance.

Although Edith's service included spiritual guidance and duties as a minister of her own church from the 1940s into the 1970s, the service that stands out most clearly both to me and many of her faithful friends and students is her work as a healer both in and out of trance. This includes healing of the body and mind.

After a session with Edith and the master guides working through her, home remedies would often be added to the therapy given on her healing table. For years I have used a simple homemade chest rub for colds and flu recommended by Nadai that consists of two parts camphor, two parts olive oil and one part eucalyptus. The decongestant effect is amazing, and when used just before bedtime, it stimulates a healing sweat that helps drive out poisons.

For sore throats the guidance would be to mix honey with glycerin. For sore, strained muscles or an aching back the remedy was a compress of castor oil covered by a wet flannel cloth and heated for an hour by a wet heat source such as a hot water bottle. To reduce stress and detoxify the body, the injunction was to take one to two Epsom salts baths per week. Many other healing suggestions acted as a self-help adjunct to the almost miraculous work Edith performed, assisted by the team of masters she worked with.

On the surface, the healing technique might take on the appearance of a one-hour, deep total-body massage combined with an energy healing similar to Touch for Health therapy or polarity healing. This is a dramatic understatement of the value and transforming effect of this work, like comparing a Rolls Royce to a tricycle.

As an example, in the early 1980s I experienced a severe financial crisis when the company I then owned collapsed during the recession that was then overtaking our economy. The business failure left me emotionally crippled, and this soon manifested in an acute arthritic attack on virtually every joint in my body. It would take me up to thirty minutes to get out of bed in the morning, and the pain of standing was excruciating. The constant pain increased my emotional stress, perpetuating the negative cycle of the condition.

I visited Edith many times over the next few months and the master Nadai did most of the healing work through Edith. The healing experience felt like the toxic condition was being drained from my body bit by bit. During this process I took no conventional medication and supplemented my diet with flower essences to help strengthen my immune system. I was also encouraged to meditate and pray each day, seeing myself whole and healthy. In this way the cause behind the effect, the thought behind the illness, was slowly changed. Within six months the condition was totally gone and there has been no recurrence.

This and many other sessions with Edith and the masters that use her as an instrument in the service of mankind slowly molded my life and helped me to achieve an all-absorbing faith in the power of the infinite wisdom, love and power that has created and rules and is all that is — the same spirit that lives within each of us. It also showed me how to live life abundantly in body, mind and spirit.

This is typical of the success Edith's work with the masters has provided for thousands of people blessed by her dedication. One healing that stands out is that of Jim Hyden, a salesman from London, England. He had endured constant headaches and could not sleep. While Edith and others visited with him in London, she found that he was possessed by a dark entity. The entity attacked Edith during her sleep and she wrestled with it, breaking its control. In the morning she found that Jim was healed and fine.

Edith has always represented the ideal rather than set herself up as an idol. If body, mind and soul can manifest eternal expressions of life, they would be displayed in a consistent and reliable fashion through compassion, kindness, humility, nonjudgment, understanding, tolerance, selflessness, harmony, gentleness and most of all, unconditional love. These are the ideals that I and many, many others have been blessed to witness through Edith Bruce in the simplest of ways over the years. They have never deviated, but have become deeper and more sublime as time went on.

I have often had the experience of feeling uplifted by merely approaching her home. Yes, anticipation was a factor, but this was something more palpable. I believe the light that shines from one who lives the Christ life radiates out in all directions, sending out its healing influence to all who are receptive whether they are aware of the source or not. Such is the power of this great soul.

Edith is truly indicative of a devoted follower and teacher of the Master Jesus and has lived the life He taught in every way. The contents of this book are a simple compilation of the teachings of the Great Brotherhood/Sisterhood of Light given through Edith Bruce for over sixty years. No matter what spiritual faith, belief, creed, religious persuasion or even doubts about the meaning of life that one might harbor, the deep love and truth written within these pages cannot fail to strike a familiar nerve center within the deepest part of one's being, saying, "Here is refreshment, here is guidance for a soul thirsting after truth and the right use of the laws of love-righteousness!"

— *John McIntosh, author of* The Millennium Tablets

❖

In the early sixties, while spending some time in Aberdeen, Scotland, and during my research into metaphysics, I was invited to attend a Spiritualist service where the Rev. Edith Bruce was administering her Sunday service. I decided to sit in the back row with my family, thereby allowing me to leave the service should I wish. I discovered that this vibrant lady was delivering messages to individuals present from departed relatives and friends. These were random, spiritually guided messages.

Some thirty minutes later I had decided to leave when I heard her voice from the platform saying, "Please, sir, do not leave. I have a message for you. Kindly sit and wait a few moments." My turn soon came for this message. "There is a North American Indian behind you, and he has been there for a while. He says he is your spiritual guide and that one day you will settle in his country — and further, he will speak to you in the near future through another channel." Naturally, being an investigator at the time, I took this message rather lightly, but kept an open mind.

Edith Bruce's message was eventually proven right. On one of my further investigations in London, the North American Indian guide mentioned spoke to me through a Queen's psychic, Lilian Bailey (since passed on). In addition, I have now been settled as foretold in the city of Toronto since 1979, something that had never entered my mind and which I had thought impossible at the time I first heard it.

Many thanks to Rev. Edith Bruce, who has become a very close friend to me and my family since 1980. Who can doubt her sincerity and the divine powers bestowed on her?

> — *Bill Williams, lecturer and speaker*
> *on the human potential*

I had the pleasure of first meeting Rev. Edith Bruce in 1971 when driving with her to the home of a mutual friend. We had no sooner started on our journey when Edith commenced the first of many psychic readings she would give to me.

She began to speak of things, events and people who were part of my life past and present and who were completely unknown to anyone else but me. This was my first introduction to someone like Edith, and I found the experience very unnerving. It was the beginning of a friendship and a respect for Edith that grew and developed over the years.

I have observed, and listened to testimony from, people who, through Edith's love and spirituality, were able to overcome despair, pain and insecurity. Through her healings Edith has helped her clients to feel better, acquire more energy, become more productive and generally enjoy life and see it from a more relaxed perspective. People become more positive from their contact with the spiritual guidance that flows through Edith and soon notice a major improvement in both their physical and behavioral well-being.

Edith's energy and love provide support and a steady resource during personal crises. I have observed ill people become physically and mentally stronger, enabling them to face their difficulties more efficiently.

I am now seventy-one years of age, and over the last twenty-five years Edith has helped open my awareness to the reality of the spiritual world. She has had a major impact on my personal ability to deal with the challenge of life. She has also helped me heal a major personal illness and enabled me to be a more productive and contributing member of society.

— *James W. Rockley, businessman*

It was a privilege for me to observe a dramatic healing which occurred through the ministrations of the Rev. Edith Bruce. A medical doctor declared that an alcoholic man was terminally ill and had three months to live. The man in question, although normally slender, was bloated to the point of resembling a nine-month pregnancy. The liver and pancreas were severely damaged. After a one-and-a-half-hour session in the healing room with Edith, the man emerged with the swelling totally removed. He had followup treatments for three months and then returned to work, well and healthy for ten years before retirement.

— *Florence I. Patterson, friend*

BOOK MARKET

A reader's guide to the extraordinary books we publish, print and market for your enLightenment.

◆ NEW!

ARCTURUS PROBE
José Arguelles

A poetic depiction of how the Earth was seeded by beings from the Arcturus system of three million years ago. The author of *The Mayan Factor* tells how Atlantis and Elysium were played out on Mars and implanted into Earth consciousness. Illustrated.

$14.95 Softcover   ISBN 0-929385-75-6

GUARDIANS OF THE FLAME
Tamar George

Channeled drama of a golden city in a crystal land and tells of Atlantis, the source of humanity's ritual, healing, myth and astrology. Life in Atlantis over 12,000 years ago through the eyes of Persephone, a magician who can become invisible. A story you'll get lost in.

$14.95 Softcover   ISBN 0-929385-76-4

THE MILLENNIUM TABLETS
John McIntosh

Twelve tablets containing 12 powerful secrets, yet only 2 opened. The Lightbearers and Wayshowers will pave the way, dispelling darkness and allowing the opening of the 10 remaining tablets to humanity, thus beginning the age of total freedom.

$14.95 Softcover   ISBN 0-929385-78-0

◆ OLDER CLASSICS

THE TRANSFORM-ATIVE VISION
José Arguelles

Reprint of his 1975 tour de force, which prophesied the Harmonic Convergence as the "climax of matter," the collapse of materialism. Follows the evolution of the human soul in modern times by reviewing its expressions through the arts and philosophers.

$14.95 Softcover 364p   ISBN 0-9631750-0-9

OUT-OF-BODY EXPLORATION
Jerry Mulvin

Techniques for traveling in the Soul Body to achieve absolute freedom and experience truth for oneself. Discover reincarnation, karma and your personal spiritual path.

$8.95 Softcover 87p   ISBN 0-941464-01-6

VOICES OF SPIRIT
Charles H. Hapgood

The author discusses 15 years of work with Elwood Babbit, the famed channel. Will fascinate both the curious sceptic and the believer. Includes complete transcripts.

$13.00 Softcover 350p   ISBN 1-881343-00-6

THE SEDONA VORTEX GUIDEBOOK
by 12 channels

200-plus pages of channeled, never-before-published information on the vortex energies of Sedona and the techniques to enable you to use the vortexes as multidimensional portals to time, space and other realities.

ISBN 0-929385-25-X

$14.95 Softcover 236p

NEW!
GALAXY SEVEN
A novel by
Joseph David Collins

Various unrelated people establish contact with space visitors. As they start to go public, a secret, insidious government agency is out to silence them. A sort of cross between "Close Encounters of the Third Kind" and "The X Files."

ISBN 0-9654285-4-0

$15.95 Softcover

COLOR MEDICINE
The Secrets of Color Vibrational Healing
Charles Klotsche

A practitioner's manual for restoring blocked energy to the body systems with specific color wavelengths by the founder of "The 49th Vibrational Technique."

ISBN 0-929385-27-6

$11.95 Softcover 114p

THE NEXT DIMENSION IS LOVE
Ranoash

As speaker for a civilization whose species is more advanced, the entity describes the help they offer humanity by clearing the DNA. An exciting vision of our possibilities and future.

ISBN 0-929385-50-0

$11.95 Softcover 148p

REACH FOR US
Your Cosmic Teachers and Friends

Messages from Teachers, Ascended Masters and the Space Command explain the role they play in bringing the Divine Plan to the Earth now!

ISBN 0-929385-69-1

$14.95 Softcover 204p

CRYSTAL CO-CREATORS

A fascinating exploration of 100 forms of crystals, describing specific uses and their purpose, from the spiritual to the cellular, as agents of change. It clarifies the role of crystals in our awakening

ISBN 0-929385-40-3

$14.95 Softcover 288p